Werner Kieweg

Englische Verben sicher verwenden: Phrasal Verbs

Erklärungen – Beispiele – Übungen

MANZ VERLAG

Manz Verlag
© Ernst Klett Verlag GmbH, Stuttgart 2000
Alle Rechte vorbehalten
Muttersprachliche Beratung: Mary Ratcliffe, München
Lektorat: Harald Kotlarz, Ammerbuch
Umschlaggestaltung: Zembsch' Werkstatt, München
Illustration: Sven Palmowski, Stuttgart
Satz: Schwabenverlag AG, Ostfildern
Druck: Druckhaus Beltz, Hemsbach
Printed in Germany

ISBN 3-7863-2037-3

Vorwort

1 Was sind *phrasal verbs*?

Phrasal verbs sind Verben, die sehr wechselhafte Begleiter haben. Als Begleiter wählen sich diese Verben entweder eine Präposition oder ein Adverb und manchmal auch beides. Die Schwierigkeit beim Lernen besteht zum einen darin, dass die *phrasal verbs* ihre Begleiter ständig wechseln und dass man ihre Bedeutung auch dann nicht immer erschließen kann, wenn man die einzelnen Bestandteile kennt. In dem folgenden Beispiel wird dies deutlich. Auch wenn die Bedeutung von *break* und *up* bekannt sein sollte, lässt sich die Bedeutung der Verbindung *break up* nicht automatisch erschießen.

Jane **broke** **up** with Tom last night.

Verb + Begleiter

Jane **hat** gestern Abend mit Tom **Schluss gemacht**.

Das *phrasal verb break up* muss man also mit „Schluss machen" übersetzen.

2 Wie eng sind eigentlich die Beziehungen zwischen dem Verb und seinem Begleiter?

Wiederum sehr wechselhaft, ist die banale Antwort. Die folgende Tabelle zeigt drei Möglichkeiten:

	Beziehungen	Beispiel	Deutsche Entsprechung
1	Verb und Begleiter dürfen nicht getrennt werden: zum Beispiel *give in*	She likes quarrelling and never **gives in**.	Sie streitet gern und gibt niemals nach.
2	Verb und Begleiter müssen getrennt werden: zum Beispiel *ask ... out*	Another man **asked** her **out** last night.	Ein anderer Mann hat sie gestern Abend eingeladen.
3	Verb und Begleiter können getrennt werden, aber auch zusammenstehen: zum Beispiel *break up* oder *break ... up*	a) It was money trouble that **broke up** their friendship. b) It was money trouble that **broke** their friendship **up**.	Es war das liebe Geld, woran ihre Freundschaft zerbrach.

Auf den folgenden Seiten sind die häufigsten *phrasal verbs* mit Anwendungsbeispielen in alphabetischer Reihenfolge aufgelistet. Den Zusammenstellungen folgen Übungen, zu denen im Anhang die Lösungen zu finden sind.

A

1 Beispiel *to ask*

Phrasal verbs	Beispielsatz und Übersetzung	Deutsche Entsprechung
ask about	May I **ask** you **about** the money that you wanted to give me? Kann ich dich nach dem Geld fragen, das du mir geben wolltest?	nach etwas fragen
ask around	A: Do you know a good dentist here in town? B: No, I don't. You'll have to **ask around**. A: Kennst du hier einen guten Zahnarzt? B: Nein. Du musst dich umhören.	sich umhören

ask after	Mr Miller **asked after** you. Mr Miller wollte wissen, wie es dir geht.	jemanden fragen, wie es ihm geht
ask for	There's somebody at the door, **asking for** you. Da ist jemand an der Tür, der dich sprechen möchte.	jemanden sprechen wollen
ask for	You should have **asked** him **for** help. Du hättest ihn um Hilfe bitten sollen.	jemanden (um etwas) bitten
ask in	Don't keep him standing at the door, **ask** him **in**. Lass ihn doch nicht an der Tür stehen, bitte ihn herein!	jemanden bitten, einzutreten / hereinzukommen
ask of	May I **ask** a favour **of** you? Darf ich dich um einen Gefallen bitten?	jemanden um etwas bitten
ask out	He never **asks** me **out**. Er lädt mich niemals ein.	jemanden einladen (in ein Restaurant z.B.)
ask round	He **asked** me **round** for coffee. Er hat mich auf einen Kaffee eingeladen.	jemanden (spontan) einladen
ask to	How many people are you going to **ask to** your wedding? Wie viele Leute willst du zu deiner Hochzeit einladen?	jemanden (offiziell) einladen

Übung 1: Ergänze die fehlenden Begleiter.

1 Tom: May I ask you _____ the book that I lent you a long time ago?
   Susan: I haven't finished it yet. Can I keep it for another week or so?

2 Don't leave them standing on the doorstep – ask them _____

3 I asked _____ tea and he gave me coffee.

4 I've asked some friends _____ for dinner. Is that okay?

5 He wanted to ask her _____, but he didn't dare.

6 We won't ask many people _____ our wedding. We'll save the money for a car.

7 There's somebody on the phone, asking _____ Mum.

8	Tom: Mrs Miller asked _____ you. Susan: Oh, how kind of her.
9	Mary has been asked _____ to a dance on Saturday.
10	All I ask _____ you is that you (should) make your own bed.

Übung 2: Versuche die deutsche Entsprechung zu den folgenden Sätzen zu finden.

	Englisch	Deutsch
1	If you go by car in this weather, you're asking for trouble. Why don't you take the train?	
2	Ask him his name.	
3	Is he really asking for an old car like that?	

Weitere wichtige *phrasal verbs*, die mit „a" beginnen

Phrasal verbs	Beispielsatz und Übersetzung	Deutsche Entsprechung
add to	*We've got to add another room to the house.* *We're going to have another baby.* Wir müssen ein weiteres Zimmer anbauen. Wir bekommen wieder Nachwuchs.	etwas anbauen bzw. erweitern
add up	*Add these figures up and see what the total is.* Addiere diese Zahlen und schau' nach, was herauskommt.	addieren, zusammenzählen
agree on sth.	*The bike is great, but we haven't agreed on the price yet.* Das Rad ist großartig, aber wir haben uns noch nicht über den Preis geeinigt.	sich über etwas einigen

agree with	Dad says it's too risky and I **agree with** him. Papa sagt, es sei zu riskant, und ich stimme ihm zu.	jemandem zustimmen
argue about	They're always **arguing about** unimportant matters. Sie streiten sich immer über unwichtige Angelegenheiten.	mit jemandem über etwas streiten
argue against	Why do you always **argue against** me? Warum widersprichst du mir dauernd?	jemandem widersprechen

Übung 3:
Welche Übersetzung ist richtig?
Setze ein Kreuz in das richtige Kästchen.

Beispielsätze		**Übersetzungen**
1 We've got to add to another bedroom for the kids at the back.	☐	Die Kinder müssen ein weiteres Schlafzimmer an der Rückseite anbauen.
	☐	Wir müssen an der Rückseite eine weiteres Schlafzimmer für die Kinder anbauen.
2 He added the figures up and then told me the total.	☐	Er zählte die Zahlen zusammen und sagte mir dann das Ergebnis.
	☐	Er zählte die Rechnungen zusammen und dann erzählte er mir alles.
3 We agreed on a price for the bike.	☐	Wir einigten uns auf einen Preis für das Rad.
	☐	Wir einigten uns auf ein Rad als Preis.
4 Let us not argue about whether it is safe to climb a mountain in this weather.	☐	Wir brauchen uns nicht zu streiten, dass es sicher ist, bei diesem Wetter einen Berg zu besteigen.
	☐	Wir brauchen uns nicht zu streiten, wie sicher es ist, bei diesem Wetter einen Berg zu besteigen.

B

1 Beispiel *to break*

*My car **broke down** this morning.*

Phrasal verbs	Beispielsatz und Übersetzung	Deutsche Entsprechung
break down	*My car **broke down** this morning.* Heute Morgen hatte ich eine Autopanne.	eine Panne haben
break down	*In the afternoon somebody **broke down** my front door.* Am Nachmittag hat jemand meine Haustür eingeschlagen.	einschlagen, zertrümmern
break into	*Someone **broke into** my flat while I was at work.* Jemand brach in meine Wohnung ein, während ich in der Arbeit war.	(in ein Gebäude) eindringen / einbrechen
break out of	*It was somebody who had **broken out of** prison.* Es war jemand, der aus dem Gefängnis ausgebrochen ist.	ausbrechen (aus einem Gefängnis)
break off	*Tom and Sue eventually **broke off** their engagement.* Tom und Sue haben schließlich ihre Verlobung aufgelöst.	abbrechen, auflösen
break up with	*Tom **broke up with** me.* Tom hat mit mir Schluss gemacht.	mit jemandem Schluss machen

Übung 1: Ergänze die fehlenden *phrasal verbs*.

	Deutsch	Englisch
1	Mein Moped gab seinen Geist auf und ich musste zu Fuß in die Schule gehen.	My moped _____ and I had to walk to school.
2	Hast du schon gehört? Susan hat mit Bob gestern Abend Schluss gemacht.	Have you heard the news? Susan _____ Bob last night.
3	Jemand brach in meine Wohnung ein, während ich im Kino war.	Somebody _____ my flat while I was at the movies.
4	Gestern hatte ich auf der Autobahn eine Panne und musste den Abschleppdienst verständigen.	Yesterday my car _____ on the motorway. I had to call the breakdown service.
5	Gestern brachen drei Männer aus dem Gefängnis aus.	Three men _____ prison yesterday.
6	Ich konnte in mein Auto nicht einsteigen, weil der Türgriff abgebrochen war.	I couldn't get into my car, because the door handle had _____.

2   Beispiel *to be*

about — up — up — around — through — **be** — out — on — after — off — in

*Mrs Miller **is** not **in** today. Can I take a message?*

Phrasal verbs	Beispielsatz und Übersetzung	Deutsche Entsprechung
be around	*Mike is around somewhere.* Mike muss irgendwo in der Nähe sein.	in der Nähe sein
be about	*What is your new book about?* Von was handelt dein neues Buch?	handeln von
be about to	*Nick was about to leave when his friend arrived.* Nick wollte gerade gehen, als sein Freund ankam.	gerade etwas tun wollen
be after	*The police are after me.* Die Polizei ist hinter mir her.	hinter jemandem her sein, jemanden verfolgen
be in	*Mrs Miller is not in today. Can I take a message?* Mrs Miller ist heute nicht da. Kann ich ihr etwas ausrichten?	da sein
be off	*Make sure the lights are off before you leave.* Vergewissere dich, dass die Lichter ausgeschaltet sind, bevor du weggehst.	ab-/ausgeschaltet sein
be on	*What's on tonight?* Was ist heute Abend geboten / los? *What's on television tonight?* Was gibts' heute Abend im Fernsehen?	los sein, geboten sein; (im Fernsehen) zu sehen sein
be out	*Mrs Miller is out. Can I take a message?* Mrs Miller ist nicht da. Kann ich etwas ausrichten?	nicht da sein
be through	*I don't want to see you again. We're through.* Ich möchte dich nicht mehr sehen. Wir sind fertig miteinander.	die Beziehungen zu jemandem abbrechen, mit jemandem fertig sein, nichts mehr wissen wollen
be up	*Don't worry about ringing me up, I'm often up late.* Sie können mich anrufen. Ich bin oft lange auf.	auf sein, wach sein

Übung 2:
Verbinde die Zahlen mit den entsprechenden Buchstaben.

We're through.	A
She's not in today.	B
She's out at the moment.	C
The plane is about to take off.	D
What's it about?	E
He's only after your money.	F
The water is off.	G
What's on TV?	H
Is Tom around?	I
Are you still up?	J

1	Ist Tom in der Nähe?
2	Das Wasser ist abgedreht.
3	Bist du noch auf?
4	Das Flugzeug startet gerade.
5	Sie ist heute nicht im Büro.
6	Wir sind fertig miteinander.
7	Er ist nur hinter deinem Geld her.
8	Sie ist momentan nicht da.
9	Was gibt es im Fernsehen?
10	Wovon handelt es?

3   Beispiel *to bring*

*Alcohol **brought** him **down**.*

Phrasal verbs	Beispielsatz und Übersetzung	Deutsche Entsprechung
bring about	*Alcohol has **brought about** lots of problems.* Der Alkohol hat viele Probleme mit sich gebracht.	mit sich bringen
bring along	*I told you to **bring** your pyjamas **along**.* I habe ihnen gesagt, dass Sie ihren Schlafanzug mitbringen sollen.	mitbringen
bring down	*Alcohol **brought** him **down**.* Der Alkohol hat ihn zu Fall gebracht.	jemanden zu Fall bringen, jemanden fertig machen
bring round	*He has fainted. We must try to **bring** him **round**.* Er hat das Bewusstsein verloren. Wir müssen versuchen, ihn zurückzuholen.	zu sich bringen; vorbeibringen, mitbringen
bring up	*He was **brought up** in an orphanage here in London.* Er wuchs in einem Waisenhaus hier in London auf.	erziehen, aufziehen, aufwachsen

Übung 3: Kreuze den passenden Begleiter an.

1 My parents both died in a car crash. So I was brought _____ by my grandparents.

| in | round | about | up | down | back |

2 The books are due back tomorrow[1]. I should take them _____ to the library.

| in | round | about | up | down | back |

3 After he had fainted we did our best to bring him _____.

| in | round | about | up | down | back |

4 His drinking and driving brought him _____.

| in | round | about | up | down | back |

5 (At the police station) The policeman brought _____ two boys he had caught stealing.

| in | round | about | up | down | back |

| 6 | Computers have brought _____ many changes in our lives. |

| in | round | about | up | down | back |

| 7 | Bring your running shoes _____, we'll get some exercise. |

| in | round | along | up | down | back |

| 8 | He left her last summer. She has to bring _____ three children on her own. |

| in | round | about | up | down | back |

| 9 | His drinking brought _____ disaster[2] on the whole family. |

| in | round | about | up | down | back |

| 10 | He opened all the windows in the hope of bringing her _____. |

| in | round | about | up | down | back |

[1] Die Ausleihfrist der Bücher läuft morgen ab.
[2] disaster = Unheil

4 Weitere *phrasal verbs*, die mit „b" beginnen

Phrasal verbs	Beispielsatz und Übersetzung	Deutsche Entsprechung
back up	I *back up* my files regularly. Ich sichere meine Dateien regelmäßig. *Tell them what really happened. I'll back you up.* Sage ihnen, was wirklich geschehen ist. Ich werde dich unterstützen.	sichern (Computer); unterstützen, untermauern
blow up	They *blew up* the old bridge. Sie haben die alte Brücke gesprengt/in die Luft gejagt.	sprengen, in die Luft jagen
blow up	*Blow up* some balloons for the party, won't you? Blase ein paar Ballons für die Party auf.	aufblasen

brush up	If you go to England, you'd better **brush up** your English. Wenn du nach England fährst, solltest du dein Englisch auffrischen.	(Wissen) auffrischen
bump into	I **bumped into** an old friend of mine. Ich habe zufällig einen alten Freund von mir getroffen.	jemanden zufällig treffen
bump into	I **bumped into** the door and hurt my knee. Ich rannte gegen die Tür und verletzte mein Knie.	gegen etwas stoßen, rennen
burn down	Lightning struck our barn last night. It **burned down** completely. Ein Blitz traf gestern Abend unsere Scheune. Sie brannte vollständig nieder.	niederbrennen, abbrennen
burn up	The rocket **burned up** in the atmosphere. Die Rakete verglühte in der Atomsphäre.	verbrennen, verglühen

Übung 4:
Wie würdest du die folgenden Sätze auf Englisch formulieren?

	German	Englisch
1	Wenn du dein Englisch nicht auffrischst, wird dich niemand verstehen.	
2	Sei vorsichtig. Du könntest gegen die Mauer fahren.	
3	Sichere deine Dateien. Du könntest sie sonst verlieren.	
4	Stell' das Rauchen sofort ein. Oder möchtest du das Haus in die Luft jagen?	
5	Der Meteorit (meteorite) verglühte in der Atmosphäre.	
6	Blase den Ballon nicht zu sehr auf. Er könnte platzen.	

C

1 Beispiel *to call*

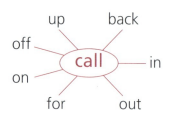

Phrasal verbs	Beispielsatz und Übersetzung	Deutsche Entsprechung
call back	Mrs White is not in today. Can she **call** you **back**? Mrs White ist heute nicht im Büro. Kann sie Sie zurückrufen?	jemanden telefonisch zurückrufen
call for	Yes, dear! I'll **call for** you at 6 o'clock. Ja, Liebling! Ich werde dich um 6 Uhr abholen.	jemanden abholen
call off	The match has been **called off**. There's no need to hurry. Das Spiel wurde abgesagt. Wir brauchen uns jetzt nicht mehr beeilen.	ein Spiel oder eine Veranstaltung absagen

call out	*I can't find Mary. I have had her name **called out** several times.* Ich kann Mary nicht finden. Ich ließ sie schon mehrere Male ausrufen.	jemanden ausrufen lassen
call up	***Call** me **up** when you're ready.* Ruf mich an, wenn du fertig bist.	jemanden anrufen
call on	*Why don't you **call on** my brother when you're in London.* Warum schaust du nicht bei meinem Bruder vorbei, wenn du in London bist?	jemanden kurz besuchen, bei jemandem vorbeischauen

Übung 1: Ergänze die fehlenden Sätze.

(Tom ist im Büro und bekommt gerade einen Anruf von seiner Freundin.)

Tom: "Good morning. Can I help you?"

Sue: "Hello, Tom. It's me. Sue."

Tom: "Hello, dear. _____(1)? I'm very busy at the moment.
(Kann ich dich zurückrufen?)

Sue: "Okay. _____(2). Cheerio!"
(Ruf' mich so bald wie möglich an.)

(An hour later)

Tom: "Tom. What's up, dear?"

Sue: "_____(3). So what shall we do tonight?
(Man hat gerade das Tennismatch abgesagt.)

Tom: "_____(4)"
(Wir können nach dem Abendessen kurz mal bei Anne vorbeischauen)

Sue: "Good idea! Perhaps we can ask her out for a drink."

Tom: "Okay then. _____(5). Cheerio!"
(Hol' mich bitte um 5 Uhr ab.)

4 Weitere *phrasal verbs*, die mit "c" beginnen

Phrasal verbs	Beispielsatz und Übersetzung	Deutsche Entsprechung
catch up with	Hurry up! They're far ahead of us. We've got to **catch up with** them. Beeile dich! Sie sind uns weit voraus. Wir müssen sie einholen.	jemanden einholen, mit jemandem aufschließen
catch up with	I was ill and missed four weeks of school. Now I've got lots to **catch up with**. Ich war krank und habe vier Wochen Unterricht verpasst. Nun muss ich viel aufholen.	(versäumten Stoff in der Schule) aufholen oder nachlernen
calm down	He was very upset. I could hardly **calm** him **down**. Er war sehr verärgert. Ich konnte ihn kaum beruhigen.	beruhigen
care for	My grandmother came out of hospital last week. Now we've got to **care for** her at home. Meine Großmutter wurde letzte Woche aus dem Krankenhaus entlassen. Nun müssen wir uns zu Hause um sie kümmern.	sich um jemanden kümmern, jemanden versorgen
carry out	He never **carries out** any orders. Er führt niemals Befehle aus.	(einen Befehl) ausführen
carry on	The doctor told him to stop smoking. But he **carried on**. Der Arzt sagte ihm, dass er das Rauchen aufgeben sollte. Aber er rauchte weiter.	weitermachen, fortführen
check in	The registration desk is over there. You can **check in** now. Die Rezeption ist dort drüben. Sie können sich jetzt anmelden.	sich anmelden, einchecken
check into	You should **check into** the hotel by 9 o'clock at the latest. Du solltest spätestens gegen neun Uhr im Hotel einchecken.	sich anmelden, einchecken
check out	Don't forget to leave your room key at the front desk when you **check out**. Vergiss nicht deinen Schlüssel an der Rezeption abzugeben, wenn du abfährst.	abreisen (Hotel)
cheer up	You are looking so cross. How can I **cheer** you **up**? Du schaust so böse. Wie kann ich dich aufheitern?	aufheitern, bessere Laune bekommen

clear up	Could you **clear up** the mess in your room, please? Könntest du dein Zimmer aufräumen?	(ein Zimmer) aufräumen
close down	Last week another shop in the precinct **closed down**. Letzte Woche schloss ein weiteres Geschäft in der Fußgängerzone.	(einen Laden) schließen
count on	I'm **counting on** you to help me. Ich verlasse mich auf dich, dass du mir hilfst.	sich verlassen auf, zählen auf
cut down	The essay is too long. **Cut** it **down** a bit. Der Aufsatz ist zu lang. Kürze ihn ein wenig.	kürzen
cut off	I **cut off** a big piece of meat and gave it to him. Ich schnitt ein großes Stück Fleisch ab und gab es ihm.	(ein Stück) abschneiden

Übung 2:
Welche Übersetzung ist richtig? Setze ein Kreuz in das richtige Kästchen.

	Englisch		German
1	My school report was rather poor. Mum tried to cheer me up.	☐	Mein Zeugnis war ziemlich schlecht. Mutter versuchte mich zu beruhigen.
		☐	Meine Mutter versuchte mich aufzuheitern.
2	She said that I had to catch up with a lot after 6 weeks in hospital.	☐	Sie sagt, dass ich viel aufzuholen habe nach 6 Wochen im Krankenhaus.
		☐	Sie sagte, dass ich viel aufzuholen hatte nach 6 Wochen im Krankenhaus.
3	Father was very angry when he saw my report. But Mum tried to calm him down.	☐	Vater war sehr verärgert, als er mein Zeugnis sah. Aber Mutter versuchte ihn zu beruhigen.
		☐	Aber Mutter versuchte ihn zu trösten.
4	She asked him to stop shouting, but he carried on.	☐	Sie bat ihn, nicht mehr zu schreien, aber er schrie weiter.
		☐	Sie bat ihn, nicht mehr zu schreien, aber er schrie noch mehr.
5	He said he would cut down my pocket money.	☐	Er sagte, er würde mein Taschengeld streichen.
		☐	Er sagte, er würde mein Taschengeld kürzen.

Übung 3: Kannst du auf Englisch sagen, was dir der Lehrer mitteilte?

	Der Englischlehrer sagte mir, dass …	**The English teacher told me …**
1	… ich meinen Aufsatz ein bisschen kürzen solle.	_____
2	… ich mehr lernen solle, um den Anschluss an die anderen Schüler zu bekommen.	_____
3	… ich bessere Laune bekommen sollte.	_____
4	… ich mich auf ihn verlassen könne.	_____
5	… ich meinen Schreibtisch aufräumen sollte.	_____

D

1 Beispiel *to drop*

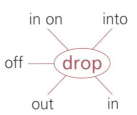

*Look, she's **dropped off** in front of the TV.*

Phrasal verbs	Beispielsatz und Übersetzung	Deutsche Entsprechung
drop in	*Please try to **drop in** when you're in town, will you?* Schau doch mal vorbei, wenn du in der Stadt bist. Okay?	bei jemandem kurz vorbeikommen
drop in on	*Let's **drop in on** Mary and Sue, shall we?* Schauen wir doch mal kurz bei Mary und Sue vorbei. Okay?	bei jemandem vorbeischauen
drop out	*Mike isn't at university anymore. He **dropped out**.* Mike ist nicht mehr an der Uni. Er hat sein Studium abgebrochen.	(ein Studium, eine Arbeit) abbrechen

drop off	I can take these letters to the post office. I'll **drop** them **off** on my way home. Ich kann diese Briefe zur Post bringen. Ich werfe sie auf meinem Weg nach Hause ein.	(einen Brief) einwerfen
drop off	I can give you a lift and **drop** you **off** at the post office. Ich kann dich im Auto mitnehmen und an der Post absetzen.	absetzen (Fahrgast)
drop off	Look, she's **dropped off** in front of the TV. Schau, sie ist vor dem Fernseher eingenickt.	einnicken

Übung 1: Ergänze die fehlenden *phrasal verbs*.

	Deutsch	Englisch
1	Ich möchte, dass du bei Oma vorbeischaust. Sie hat heute Geburtstag.	I want you to _____ Grandma. It's her birthday today.
2	Sie kommt immer bei mir vorbei, wenn sie nach Hause geht.	She always _____ on her way home.
3	Sage ihr aber nicht, dass Tom sein Studium hingeschmissen hat. Sie wäre schockiert.	Don't tell her that Tom has _____ of university. She would be shocked.
4	Um diese Zeit nickt sie oftmals vor dem Fernseher ein.	This time of day she often _____ in front of the telly.
5	Kannst du mich mitnehmen und am Bahnhof absetzen?	Could you give me a lift and _____ me _____ at the station?
6	Und bringe diese Briefe zum Postamt. Vater hat vergessen, sie heute Morgen einzuwerfen.	And then take these letters to the post office. Dad forgot to _____ them _____ this morning.

Weitere *phrasal verbs*, die mit „d" beginnen

Phrasal verbs	Beispielsatz und Übersetzung	Deutsche Entsprechung
dash away / off	*I must **dash away** / **off** now, I'm already late for the meeting.* Ich muss jetzt schnell weg. Ich komme schon zu spät zur Sitzung.	schnell einen Ort verlassen, davonjagen
deal out	***Deal out** eight cards to each player.* Teile an jeden Spieler acht Karten aus.	(Spielkarten) austeilen
deal with	*Who's going to **deal with** this problem?* Wer wird sich um dieses Problem kümmern?	sich um etwas kümmern, sich einer Sache annehmen
do about	*I can't **do** anything **about** it.* Ich kann da nichts tun./Ich kann da nicht helfen.	tun, helfen
do for	*This old car will **do for** getting around until we can afford a new one.* Dieses alte Auto reicht zum Herumfahren, bis wir uns ein neues leisten können.	es reicht aus, es erfüllt seinen Zweck
done for	*I'm going to bed. I'm **done for**.* Ich gehe ins Bett. Ich bin geschafft.	geschafft sein, sehr müde sein
do over (AE)	*Your essay is full of mistakes. You'd better **do** it **over**.* Dein Aufsatz ist voller Fehler. Du solltest ihn überarbeiten.	(einen Aufsatz) überarbeiten
do to	*What have you **done to** this poor cat?* Was hast du dieser armen Katze angetan?	jemandem etwas antun
do up	***Do up** your coat. It's cold outside.* Knöpfe deinen Mantel zu. Es ist kalt draußen.	(ein Kleidungsstück) zuknöpfen
do without	*I can't afford a motorbike. So I guess I'll just have to **do without**.* Ich kann mir kein Motorrad leisten. Ich schätze, ich muss ohne eins auskommen.	ohne etwas auskommen
draw back	*I **drew back** when I saw the blood on the ground.* Ich wich zurück, als ich das Blut am Boden sah.	zurückweichen

dress up	*He went to the party **dressed up** as a vampire.* Er ging auf die Party als Vampir verkleidet.	sich verkleiden
dress up	*What kind of party is it? Will we have to **dress up**?* Was für eine Party ist das? Müssen wir uns schön anziehen?	sich schön / fein anziehen
drift apart	*After ten years of marriage, they began to **drift apart**.* Nach zehn Jahren Ehe gingen sie immer mehr ihre eigenen Wege.	seine eigenen Wege gehen
drink to	*Let us **drink to** the happy pair.* Lasst uns auf das glückliche Paar anstoßen.	auf jemanden anstoßen
drive up	*A police car **drove up** and stopped in front of our house.* Ein Polizeiauto fuhr vor und hielt vor unserem Haus.	vorfahren

Übung 2: Was sagst du in den folgenden Situationen?

	Situationsbeschreibung	Was würdest du sagen?
1	Eine Freundin hat ihre Bluse zu weit geöffnet.	_____
2	Jemand möchte zu elegant gekleidet zu einer ganz normalen Party gehen.	_____
3	Jemand weiß nicht, in welcher Maske er auf einen Faschingsball gehen soll.	_____
4	Jemand muss zum Flughafen und du fährst dort vorbei und würdest ihn mitnehmen.	_____
5	Jemand weiß nicht, wie viele Karten ein Spieler beim Schafskopf bekommt.	_____
6	Du teilst jemandem mit, dass du dich um ein bestimmtes Problem kümmerst.	_____
7	Jemand hat einen sehr fehlerhaften Brief geschrieben.	_____
8	Während eines Konzerts ist jemand kurz vor dem Einschlafen.	_____
9	Jemand sollte seine Eltern wieder besuchen.	_____
10	Du möchtest jemand davon abbringen, die Schule aufzugeben.	_____
11	Du möchtest auf den Geburtstag deiner Großmutter anstoßen.	_____
12	Du musst ganz schnell verschwinden.	_____

E

1 Beispiel *to end*

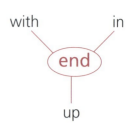

Phrasal verbs	Beispielsatz und Übersetzung	Deutsche Entsprechung
end up	I've told you again and again that you'll **end up** in prison. Ich habe dir immer wieder gesagt, dass du im Gefängnis landen würdest.	enden, landen
end up	He **ended up** as a criminal. Er wurde schließlich ein Krimineller.	(schließlich) werden
end up	We arrived at Rome airport, but our luggage **ended up** in Paris. Wir kamen am Flughafen von Rom an, aber unser Gepäck landete in Paris.	landen, ankommen
end in	Their marriage **ended in** divorce. Ihre Ehe endete mit einer Scheidung.	enden
end with	The film **ended with** the hero dying. Die Film endete mit dem Tod des Helden.	enden mit

Übung 1:

Formuliere deine Vorhersagen zu den angegebenen Situationen und verwende dabei die *phrasal verbs* aus der Übersicht.

	Situations	Formuliere deine Vorhersagen.
1	Somebody keeps stealing things from the supermarket.	_____
2	Somebody is a heavy smoker. He doesn't listen to the doctor's advice.	_____
3	A married man keeps looking at other women. His wife is very angry about that.	_____
4	Somebody is working too hard. He doesn't look well.	_____

Weitere *phrasal verbs*, die mit „e" beginnen

Phrasal verbs	Beispielsatz und Übersetzung	Deutsche Entsprechung
eat away	*Some parts of the car have been **eaten away** by rust.* Einige Teile des Autos sind vom Rost zerfressen.	etwas zerfressen
eat up	*Come on, **eat** it **up**. Be a good girl.* Nun los, iss es auf! Sei ein braves Mädchen.	aufessen
eat out	*I'm too tired to cook tonight. Why don't we **eat out**?* Ich bin heute Abend zu müde zum Kochen. Warum gehen wir nicht essen?	essen gehen
egg on	*He wouldn't have thrown the stones towards the police, if the other boys hadn't **egged** him **on**.* Er hätte die Polizei nicht mit Steinen beworfen, wenn die anderen Jungen ihn nicht angestachelt hätten.	jemanden anstacheln etwas zu tun

Übung 2: Ordne richtig zu.

Eat it up.	a
Don't egg them on.	b
Let's eat out tonight.	c
We're lost. Where shall we end up?	d
You'll end up in prison.	e

1	Du wirst im Gefängnis enden.
2	Wir haben uns verlaufen. Wo werden wir landen?
3	Iss auf!
4	Lasst uns heute Abend essen gehen.
5	Hör auf, sie anzustacheln.

F

1 Beispiel *to fall*

*He **fell on** the pizza as if he hadn't eaten for weeks.*

Phrasal verbs	Beispielsatz und Übersetzung	Deutsche Entsprechung
fall apart	You shouldn't buy this one. It's going to **fall apart** sooner or later. Das hier sollten Sie nicht kaufen. Das fällt über kurz oder lang auseinander.	auseinander brechen, auseinander fallen
fall away	A piece of metal has **fallen away** from the engine. Vom Motor ist ein Stück Metall abgebrochen.	abfallen, abbrechen
fall behind	Speed up! We're **falling behind**. Gib Gas! Wir fallen zurück.	(hinter jemanden) zurückfallen
fall down	I **fell down** and twisted my ankle. Ich fiel und verdrehte mein Gelenk.	fallen, stürzen
fall down	Tom's house is **falling down**. Toms Haus stürzt ein.	einstürzen
fall in	Get out of this room. The ceiling is going to **fall in**. Raus aus diesem Zimmer! Die Decke wird gleich einstürzen.	einstürzen

fall off	Last year the number of students **fell off** by ten per cent. Im letzten Jahr ging die Zahl der Studenten um zehn Prozent zurück.	zurückgehen
fall on	He **fell on** the pizza as if he hadn't eaten for weeks. Er machte sich über die Pizza her, als ob er schon seit Wochen nicht mehr gegessen hätte.	über etwas herfallen
fall out	They don't get on with each other. They are always **falling out** about something or other. Sie verstehen sich nicht gut. Sie streiten sich ständig über das eine oder andere.	streiten
fall over	Don't **fall over** the picnic basket. Stolpere nicht über den Picknickkorb.	fallen, stolpern
fall through	The plan **fell through** at the last minute. Der Plan scheiterte in der letzten Minute.	scheitern, ins Wasser fallen

Übung 1: Setze die passenden *phrasal verbs* in die Lücken ein.

1	Tim _____ one of the electric cables and hurt himself badly.	fall apart
2	I'm not riding in this old car. It's _____.	fall on
3	One of the older walkers soon _____. So we had to wait.	fall off
4	The kids _____ the cake like a pack of wolves.	fall over
5	Many people give up smoking. Therefore the production of cigarettes has _____ for the last years.	fall through
6	I wanted to go to Italy on holiday. But my plans _____ when I got ill.	fall out
7	His teeth started _____.	fall behind

Weitere *phrasal verbs*, die mit „f" beginnen

Phrasal verbs	Beispielsatz und Übersetzung	Deutsche Entsprechung
face up to	*You must face up to reality.* Du musst dich mit der Realität abfinden.	sich mit etwas abfinden
feel like	*I feel like a cup of tea.* Ich habe Lust auf eine Tasse Tee.	Lust haben auf
feel up to	*I know the accident was a terrible shock. Do you feel up to talking about it?* Ich weiß, dass der Unfall ein schwerer Schock für dich war. Bist du schon in der Lage, darüber zu sprechen?	in der Lage sein, etwas zu tun
fight back	*If he hit you, why didn't you fight back?* Wenn er dich geschlagen hat, warum hast du nicht zurückgeschlagen?	zurückschlagen, sich wehren
figure out	*The maths homework was really difficult. It took me ages to figure it out.* Die Mathe Hausaufgaben waren wirklich schwer. Ich brauchte eine Ewigkeit, um sie zu lösen.	ausrechnen, lösen
fill in	*Would you fill in this form, please?* Würden Sie bitte dieses Formular ausfüllen?	(ein Formular) ausfüllen
fill up	*Check the oil and fill her up, please.* Überprüfen Sie das Öl und volltanken, bitte.	volltanken
find out	*I tried to find out what had happened.* Ich versuchte herauszufinden, was geschehen war.	herausfinden, herausbekommen
finish off	*The children have finished off all the cake.* Die Kinder haben den ganzen Kuchen gegessen.	aufessen
fix up	*Let's fix up something for the weekend.* Lasst uns etwas für das Wochenende ausmachen.	arrangieren, ausmachen, festsetzen
fold up	*Fold up the letter and put it into the envelope.* Falte den Brief und stecke ihn in den Umschlag.	falten

Übung 2: Finde englische Entsprechungen zu den vorgegebenen Sätzen.

	Was du sagen möchtest.	Wie du es sagen kannst.
1	Versuchen Sie bitte herauszufinden, was mit dem Auto nicht stimmt.	
2	Warum muss ich dieses Formular ausfüllen?	
3	Niemand konnte das Problem bis jetzt lösen.	
4	Ich muss mich mit der Wirklichkeit abfinden und das Auto verkaufen.	
5	Bitte volltanken.	
6	Eine Tasse Kaffee wäre jetzt recht.	
7	Wir sollten etwas für die nächste Woche ausmachen.	

G

1 Beispiel *to get*

Sometimes he has problems getting his ideas across.

Phrasal verbs	Beispielsatz und Übersetzung	Deutsche Entsprechung
get across	*Sometimes he has problems getting his ideas across.* Er hat manchmal Schwierigkeiten, sich verständlich auszudrücken.	sich verständlich ausdrücken, vermitteln, klar machen
get along	*Why can't you and Mr Miller get along?* Warum kommst du mit Mr Miller nicht zurecht?	mit jemandem zurechtkommen, auskommen; vorankommen
get along with	*But everybody gets along with him just fine.* Aber jeder kommt gut mit ihm aus.	zurechtkommen, auskommen
get away	*The bank robbers got away on a stolen motorbike.* Die Bankräuber entkamen mit einem gestohlenen Motorrad.	wegkommen, entwischen, entkommen
get back	*Did you get the books back?* Hast du die Bücher zurückbekommen?	zurückkommen; etwas zurückbekommen
get in	*What time does the plane get in?* Um wie viel Uhr kommt das Flugzeug an?	ankommen, landen, einfahren
get into	*He always gets me into trouble.* Er bringt mich immer in Schwierigkeiten.	bringen in, eindringen
get off!	*Get off! Don't touch me.* Finger weg! Rühr' mich nicht an!	Finger weg!
get on	*Get on a number 5 bus ...* Steige in den Bus Nummer 5 ein ...	einsteigen (Fahrzeug)
get off	*... and then get off at the station.* ... und steige dann am Bahnhof aus.	aussteigen
get on with	*How does he get on with his colleagues?* Wie kommt er mit seinen Kollegen aus?	mit jemandem auskommen
get on with	*Stop talking and get on with your homework.* Sei still und mache mit deinen Hausaufgaben weiter!	weitermachen, fortfahren
get out	*Get out of here! The house's on fire.* Raus hier! Das Haus brennt.	Raus (hier)!
get out of	*Get out of the car and open the garage door.* Steige aus und öffne das Garagentor.	aussteigen

get over	She couldn't **get over** the early death of her father. Sie wurde mit dem frühen Tod ihres Vaters nicht fertig.	überwinden, hinwegkommen, verkraften
get through	At last I managed to **get through** to the manager. Ich konnte schließlich zum Chef durchdringen.	durchdringen, durchkommen
get together	We must **get together** some time for a drink. Wir müssen uns mal auf einen Drink treffen.	zusammenkommen, sich mit jemandem treffen
get up	What time did you **get up** this morning? Um wie viel Uhr bist du heute Morgen aufgestanden?	aufstehen
get up	**Get** me **up** at eight, would you? Weck mich um acht, ja?	wecken

Übung 1: Setze die passenden *phrasal verbs* ein.

The Hunts are going on holiday tomorrow. Mrs Hunt is a bit nervous …

1 We'll have to _____ much earlier than usual tomorrow.

2 Don't forget to _____ me _____ by six o'clock at the latest, James.

3 Mary and Tom can sit in the back of the car. They _____ well with each other at the moment, don't they?

4 Did you _____ the maps _____ from Uncle Henry? We need them.

5 Rex, _____ here! Dogs are not allowed in the kitchen.

6 We should _____ with Grandma for a drink. She'll be alone for two weeks.

7 Rex, bring it back. Look! He's _____ with the sausage rolls!

8 This dog always _____ us _____ trouble.

get together – get on – get out – get into – get up (2x) – get back – get away

2 Beispiel *to give*

Phrasal verbs	Beispielsatz und Übersetzung	Deutsche Entsprechung
give away	*He has **given away** some of his money.* Er hat einen Teil seines Geldes verschenkt.	verschenken, abgeben, verteilen
give in	*He can fight and he never **gives in**.* Er kann kämpfen und gibt niemals nach.	nachgeben
give up	*I **gave up** some of my free time to look after him.* Ich opferte einen Teil meiner Freizeit, um ihn zu versorgen.	etwas opfern, etwas aufgeben
give up	*He really should **give up** smoking.* Er sollte wirklich das Rauchen aufgeben.	mit etwas aufhören, etwas aufgeben, einstellen
give up on	*He was badly injured. The doctors had almost **given up on** him.* Er war schwer verletzt. Die Ärzte hatten ihn schon fast aufgegeben.	jemanden aufgeben

Übung 2: Übertrage die Aussagen von Mr Miller ins Deutsche.

	This is what Mr Miller told us.	Übersetzung
1	I was lucky. I had a serious accident, but I'm still alive. Now my life has been changed a lot.	
2	Doctors never should give up on people.	
3	If you think you're right, never give in.	
4	Give up some of your spare time to help people who are poor and ill.	
5	Give some of your riches away to charity[1].	
6	I gave up drinking and smoking.	

[1] charity = Wohlfahrtseinrichtung

3   Beispiel *to go*

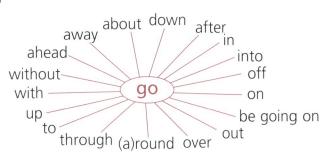

Hey! What's **going on** there?

Phrasal verbs	Beispielsatz und Übersetzung	Deutsche Entsprechung
go about	*You can't **go about** in such clothes.* Du kannst nicht in solchen Sachen herumlaufen.	herumgehen, herumlaufen
go after	*They **went after** the tiger for some days. Eventually they shot him.* Sie jagten den Tiger einige Tage lang. Und erschossen ihn dann schließlich.	jagen
go ahead	*Do you mind if I borrow your laptop? No, **go ahead**.* Macht es dir was aus, wenn ich mir dein Laptop ausleihe? Nein, nur zu.	Nur zu!
go away	***Go away.** Leave us alone.* Geh weg! Lass uns in Ruhe!	Geh weg!
go down	*Oranges have **gone down**.* Die Orangen sind billiger geworden.	billiger werden, abnehmen, zurückgehen, sinken
go in	*I want you to **go in** before it gets dark.* Ich möchte, dass du hineingehst bevor es dunkel wird.	hineingehen, reingehen
go into	*He wants to **go into** the army.* Er möchte in die Armee eintreten.	eintreten
go off	*My alarm clock **went off** in the middle of the night.* Mein Wecker läutete (plötzlich) mitten in der Nacht.	(Wecker) läuten, (plötzlich) losgehen
go on	*We can't **go on** like this.* So können wir nicht weitermachen.	weitermachen
go on	*What's **going on** here?* Was ist denn hier los?	los sein, ablaufen, vor sich gehen
go out	*How long have you been **going out** together?* Wie lange geht ihr schon miteinander?	ausgehen; mit jemandem gehen
go out	*The fire **went out** on its own.* Das Feuer erlosch von selbst.	(Feuer) ausgehen, erlöschen
go over	*Your essay is very poor. You must **go over** it, I'm afraid.* Dein Aufsatz ist sehr schwach. Du musst ihn überarbeiten, fürchte ich.	(einen Aufsatz) überarbeiten, verbessern
go (a)round	*There's a lot of flu **going (a)round** at the moment.* Zur Zeit geht die Grippe um.	(Krankheit) umgehen, verbreitet sein

go through	Let's **go through** the whole plan again. Nun lasst uns den ganzen Plan nochmals durchgehen.	durchgehen; erledigen; durchmachen; erleiden
go towards	The money will **go towards** repairing the church roof. Das Geld wird für die Reparatur des Kirchendachs aufgewandt.	(Spenden) gehen an / für, aufwenden für
go up	Tomatoes are **going up** again. Die Tomaten werden wieder teurer.	teurer werden
go with	The colour of this blouse **goes with** your hair. Die Farbe dieser Bluse passt zu deinem Haar.	zu etwas passen

Übung 3: Ergänze die fehlenden *phrasal verbs*.

German	English
Mrs Peck: "So kann das nicht weitergehen. Du arbeitest viel zu viel."	Mrs Peck: "It can't _____ like this. You work far too much."
Mr Peck: "Geh weg! Lass mich allein."	Mr Peck: "_____ Leave me alone."
Mrs Peck:" Du kannst nicht weiterhin Tag und Nacht arbeiten." Mr Peck: "Ich weiß, Schatz."	Mrs Peck: "You can't _____ working night and day." Mr Peck: "I know, dear."
Mrs Peck: "Wir sind seit einer Ewigkeit nicht mehr ausgegangen."	Mrs Peck: "We haven't _____ for ages."
Mr Peck: "Ich weiß, Liebling. Aber ich muss dieses Programm nochmals durchgehen."	Mr Peck: "I know, dear. But I've got to _____ this programme again."
Mrs Peck: "Du arbeitest seit sechs Stunden. Ich habe den Wecker läuten hören."	Mrs Peck: "You've been working for six hours. I heard the alarm clock _____."
Mr Peck: "Die Farbe deines Kostüms passt zu deinen Augen.	Mr Peck: "The colour of your costume _____ your eyes.
Mrs Peck:"Du solltest das nicht ins Lächerliche ziehen, Tom. Ich meine es ernst."	Mrs Peck: "Be serious, Tom. I mean it.

4 Beispiel *to grow*

*She has **grown into** a lovely young woman.*

Phrasal verbs	Beispielsatz und Übersetzung	Deutsche Entsprechung
grow apart	*Mary and Tom have been **growing apart**.* Mary und Tom gehen immer mehr ihre eigenen Wege.	sich auseinander leben, seinen eigenen Weg gehen
grow into	*She has **grown into** a lovely young woman.* Sie ist zu einer netten jungen Frau geworden.	werden zu
grow into	*The jacket is a bit big for you. But you'll soon **grow into** it.* Die Jacke ist für dich ein bisschen zu groß. Aber du wirst bald hineinwachsen.	hineinwachsen
grow out of	*You've **grown out of** this jacket.* Du bist aus dieser Jacke herausgewachsen.	herauswachsen
grow up	*What do you want to be when you **grow up**?* Was möchtest du werden, wenn du erwachsen bist?	erwachsen werden
grow up	*I **grew up** on a farm.* Ich bin auf einem Bauernhof aufgewachsen.	aufwachsen, groß werden

Übung 4:
Welche Bedeutung haben die *phrasal verbs* in den folgenden Sätzen?

His parents died when he was little. So he grew up in his grandparents' house.	**1**		**a**	eine schlechte Gewohnheit ablegen
I used to bite my finger nails. But I have grown out of it.	**2**		**b**	auseinander leben
He followed his father into the business. It took him a long time to grow into it.	**3**		**c**	hineinwachsen
His parents divorced when he was six. They had been growing apart.	**4**		**d**	aufwachsen

H

1 Beispiel *to hang*

*There're always youngsters **hanging about** down by the station.*

Phrasal verbs	Beispielsatz und Übersetzung	Deutsche Entsprechung
hang on to	You have come to a decision, so **hang on to** your plans. Du hast dich entschieden, darum halte an deinen Plänen fest.	festhalten an
hang about	There're always youngsters **hanging about** down by the station. Dort unten am Bahnhof lungern immer Jugendliche herum.	herumlungern

hang out	Don't **hang out** of the window. Lehn dich nicht zum Fenster hinaus.	hinauslehnen
hang out	I haven't seen him for years. Where's he **hanging out** (= living) these days? Ich habe ihn jahrelang nicht gesehen. Wo wohnt er gerade?	wohnen; sich herumtreiben
hang over	I can't sleep at night with the exam **hanging over** my head. Ich kann nachts nicht schlafen, weil das Examen über meinem Kopf schwebt.	schweben über
hang over	Don't **hang over** me while I'm working, it makes me nervous. Rück mir bei der Arbeit nicht so nahe auf die Pelle. Das macht mich nervös.	jemandem zu nahe sein, stören, auf die Pelle rücken
hang up	Don't **hang up**! I'd like to talk to you. Leg nicht auf! Ich möchte mit dir sprechen.	(den Hörer) auflegen, einhängen
hang up	**Hang up** your suit. Häng deinen Anzug auf!	(ein Kleidungsstück) aufhängen

Übung 1:

Finde passende Entgegnungen zu den Situationen in der linken Spalte und verwende dabei geeignete *phrasals verbs* aus der Aufstellung.

1	Er wirft seine Kleidungsstücke immer auf den Boden. Du möchtest das nicht.	_____
2	Er macht den ganzen Tag nichts und langweilt sich.	_____
3	Er nimmt sich etwas vor und macht es dann doch nicht.	_____
4	Beim Autofahren lehnt er sich immer aus dem Fenster.	_____

2 Beispiel *to hold*

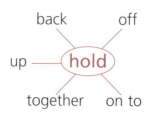

Phrasal verbs	Beispielsatz und Übersetzung	Deutsche Entsprechung
hold back	Tell me the truth. Don't **hold** anything **back**. Sagen Sie mir die Wahrheit. Verschweigen Sie nichts!	verschweigen, zurückhalten
hold back	We could hardly **hold back** our laughter. Wir konnten uns das Lachen kaum verkneifen.	(Lachen) zurückhalten, verkneifen
hold off	We managed to **hold** the crowd **off** until the police arrived. Es gelang uns, die Menge zurückzuhalten, bis die Polizei eintraf.	zurückhalten, aufhalten

hold on to	*Hold on to the rail. The driver might brake suddenly.* Halte dich an der Stange fest. Der Fahrer könnte plötzlich bremsen.	sich an etwas festhalten
hold together	*I hope the car will hold together. I can't afford a new one.* Ich hoffe, dass das Auto noch lange hält. Ich kann mir kein neues leisten.	halten
hold up	*Sorry we're late – we were held up at the office.* Tut mir Leid, wir haben uns verspätet. Wir sind im Büro aufgehalten worden.	jemanden aufhalten
hold up	*The roof is held up by these logs.* Das Dach wird von diesen Balken getragen.	stützen, tragen

Übung 2: Wie kann man das noch sagen?

1	"Tell me everything you know."	
2	"I hope your family won't split up."	
3	"The police stopped us and didn't let us go on for a long time."	
4	"Sorry, we couldn't come earlier. We had some work to do in the garage."	

Weitere *phrasal verbs*, die mit „h" beginnen

Phrasal verbs	Beispielsatz und Übersetzung	Deutsche Entsprechung
hand back	*I read the letter and then handed it back to her.* Ich las den Brief und gab ihn ihr dann zurück.	zurückgeben
hand in	*Hand your papers in at the end of the test.* Gebt eure Blätter am Ende der Prüfung ab.	(Arbeit) abgeben

hand out	Could you start **handing** these test papers **out**? Könnten Sie jetzt beginnen, die Aufgabenblätter auszuteilen?	austeilen, verteilen
hand over	The thief was **handed over** to the police. Der Dieb wurde der Polizei übergeben.	übergeben
have on	He **has** the stereo **on** all day. Er hat den ganzen Tag die Stereoanlage an.	(Radio) anhaben
have on	She **had** a nice dress **on**. Sie hatte ein nettes Kleid an.	(Kleidung) tragen, anhaben
have out	I **had** a tooth **out** the other day. Mir wurde neulich ein Zahn gezogen.	einen (Zahn) ziehen
help out	I **help out** in a supermarket on Saturdays. Samstags helfe ich in einem Supermarkt aus.	aushelfen

Übung 3:
Welche Ratschläge würdest du in den folgenden Situationen erteilen?

	Situation	Dein Ratschlag
1	Someone has had trouble with his tonsils[1] for a long time.	
2	Someone has the telly on all day.	
3	Someone has forgotten to take the test papers back to the teacher.	
4	Someone is waiting for a new secretary. You can do the job until a new secretary arrives.	

[1] *tonsils:* die Mandeln

J

Phrasal verbs	Beispielsatz und Übersetzung	Deutsche Entsprechung
jump at	She didn't hesitate and **jumped at** the offer at once. Sie zögerte nicht und nahm das Angebot sofort an.	(sofort) ergreifen (Gelegenheit), annehmen, „zuschlagen"
jump off	At the traffic light he **jumped off** the bus. An der Ampel sprang er vom Bus ab.	abspringen
jack up	You must **jack up** the car in order to change the wheels. Du musst das Auto aufbocken, um die Räder zu wechseln.	(ein Fahrzeug) aufbocken
join in	He started singing and we all **joined in**. Er begann zu singen und wir stimmten alle ein.	einstimmen, mitsingen, mitmachen
jot down	Let me **jot down** your number and I'll call you tomorrow. Lass mich schnell deine Nummer aufschreiben. Ich werde dich morgen anrufen.	(rasch) aufschreiben, notieren

Übung 1: Ergänze die fehlenden *phrasal verbs*.

1	If you actively take part in something a group is doing, you _____.
2	If you write a telephone number down quickly, you _____ the number _____.
3	If you lift a car off the ground using a jack, you _____ the car _____.
4	If you leave a train very quickly, you _____ it.

K

1 Beispiel *to keep*

Phrasal verbs	Beispielsatz und Übersetzung	Deutsche Entsprechung
keep away from	You **keep away from** my dog, will you? Lassen Sie meinen Hund in Ruhe, verstehen Sie?	jemanden in Ruhe lassen, sich von jemandem fernhalten
keep back	The police could hardly **keep back** the crowd when Michael Jackson arrived. Die Polizei konnte die Menschenmenge kaum zurückhalten, als Michael Jackson ankam.	zurückhalten; einbehalten
keep down	The employers tried to **keep** the wages **down**. Die Arbeitgeber versuchten, die Löhne niedrig zu halten.	(Löhne) niedrig halten

keep from	We should **keep** the bad news **from** her. Wir sollten die schlechte Nachricht von ihr fernhalten.	etwas von jemandem fernhalten, jemanden nicht belasten mit etwas
keep from	She **kept** him **from** committing suicide. Sie hielt ihn davon ab, Selbstmord zu begehen.	jemanden von etwas abhalten
keep in	I was **kept in** for not having done my homework. Ich musste nachsitzen, weil ich meine Hausaufgaben nicht gemacht hatte.	(Schule) nachsitzen
keep off	**Keep off** the grass! Rasen nicht betreten! / Betreten des Rasens verboten!	nicht betreten, Betreten verboten; fernhalten von
keep off	Take a beach umbrella to **keep** the sun **off**. Benutze einen Sonnenschirm, um die Sonne abzuhalten.	abhalten, schützen vor
keep on	I told him to stop, but he **kept on**. Ich sagte, dass er aufhören solle, aber er machte weiter.	weitermachen, nicht aufhören
keep out	The sign says "**Keep out**" Auf dem Schild steht "Zutritt verboten"	nicht eintreten; Zutritt verboten
keep out of	I always try to **keep out of** their quarrels. Ich halte mich immer heraus, wenn sie sich streiten.	sich heraushalten, meiden, nicht betreten
keep to	Do me a favour and **keep** it **to** yourself. Tu mir einen Gefallen und behalte es für dich.	etwas für sich behalten
keep to	You should **keep to** the terms of the contract. Du solltest dich an die Bedingungen des Vertrags halten.	sich an etwas halten (Vertrag, Regel, Gesetz, Versprechen)
keep up	**Keep up** the good work. Mach weiter so!	weitermachen, durchhalten, aufrechterhalten
keep up with	Slow down! I can't **keep up with** you. Langsamer! Ich kann nicht mithalten.	mithalten, mitkommen, Schritt halten

Übung 1: Welche *phrasal verbs* passen in die Lücken?

	German	English
1	Du gehst zu schnell. Ich kann mit dir nicht mithalten.	You're going too fast. I can't _____ with you.
2	Die Firma hat einen Teil seines Lohnes einbehalten, um den Schaden zu bezahlen, den er angerichtet hatte.	The firm _____ some of his wages to pay for the damage he had done.
3	Er legte immer eine Plastikhülle über sein Auto, um den Staub abzuhalten.	He used to put a plastic cover over his car to _____ the dust _____.
4	Die Preise steigen weiter nach oben.	Prices _____ increasing.
5	In England herrscht Linksverkehr.	Traffic in Britain _____ the left.
6	Wir können mit den Joneses nicht mithalten. Sie sind reich und wir sind es nicht.	We can't _____ the Joneses. They're rich and we are not.
7	Wir konnten das Lachen kaum zurückhalten.	We could hardly _____ laughing.
8	Du solltest gefährliche Orte meiden, wenn du in New York bist.	You should _____ from dangerous places when you are in New York.
9	Erzähle es niemandem! Behalte es für dich!	Don't tell anybody. _____ it _____ yourself!
10	Die Regierung versucht gerade, die Inflation niedrig zu halten.	The government is trying to _____ inflation.

Weitere *phrasal verbs*, die mit "k" beginnen

Phrasal verbs	Beispielsatz und Übersetzung	Deutsche Entsprechung
kick off	*What time do we kick off?* Um wie viel Uhr beginnen wir das Spiel?	(ein Spiel) beginnen
kick out	*He was kicked out of college for cheating in exams.* Er flog aus dem College, weil er im Examen betrog.	hinauswerfen, (von einer Schule) fliegen
kill off	*Pollution is killing off lots of plants.* Viele Pflanzen werden durch Luftverschmutzung vernichtet.	(Pflanzen oder Tiere) ausrotten, vernichten
knock against	*I knocked my head against the doorpost.* Ich stieß mit dem Kopf gegen den Türpfosten.	gegen etwas stoßen, anschlagen
knock down / over	*He was knocked down / over by a drunken driver.* Er wurde von einem betrunkenen Fahrer umgefahren.	niederreißen, umstürzen, umfahren
knock out	*He knocked his opponent out in round 5.* Er schlug seinen Gegner in der 5. Runde k.o.	jemanden k.o. schlagen, umhauen
know about	*You can't fool me. I know about your secret.* Du kannst mich nicht zum Narren halten. Ich weiß von deinem Geheimnis.	über etwas Bescheid wissen
know apart	*The two sisters are so much alike that even their own mother hardly knows them apart.* Die beiden Schwestern sehen sich so ähnlich, dass es selbst für die eigene Mutter sehr schwer ist, sie auseinander zu halten.	unterscheiden können, auseinander halten

Übung 2: Verbinde die folgenden Sätze miteinander.

Don't cross the street here.	1		a	Otherwise they might kick you out of school.
You have to do your homework.	2		b	It might kill off all our flowers.
Don't use too much fertilizer.	3		c	Otherwise you might knock yourself out.
Stop arguing with the headmaster.	4		d	You might get knocked over by a car.
Mind your head in this doorway.	5		e	Otherwise they might keep you in.

L

1 Beispiel *to lay*

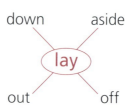

*Try to **lay aside** a few pounds each month.*

Phrasal verbs	Beispielsatz und Übersetzung	Deutsche Entsprechung
lay aside	I managed to **lay aside** a few pounds each month. Ich konnte jeden Monat einige Pfund beiseite legen.	(Geld) beiseite legen, sparen
lay down	The soldiers **laid down** their guns. Die Soldaten legten ihre Waffen nieder.	(Waffen) niederlegen; hinterlegen
lay off	There was little work in August. So I was **laid off** for four weeks. Im August gab es wenig Arbeit. Deshalb wurde ich für vier Wochen entlassen.	vorübergehend entlassen
lay out	**Lay out** the map on the table and let's have a look where to go. Breite die Karte auf dem Tisch aus und dann schauen wir, wo wir hinfahren müssen.	ausbreiten; anlegen

Übung 1: Beantworte die folgenden Fragen.

	Fragen	Deine Antworten
1	Do you lay aside any money each month?	_____
2	If you do, how much do you lay aside?	_____
3	Do you think that employers should have the right to lay off a worker?	_____
4	Do you think that workers should have the right to lay down their tools?	_____

2 **Beispiel** *to leave*

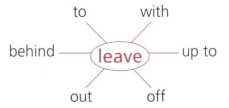

Phrasal verbs	Beispielsatz und Übersetzung	Deutsche Entsprechung
leave behind	He died last year and **left** three children **behind**. Er starb letztes Jahr und hinterließ drei Kinder.	zurücklassen, hinterlassen
leave off	**Leave off** making that noise, won't you? Schluss mit diesem Lärm, hörst du?	aufhören
leave out	You've **left out** a word in this sentence. Du hast ein Wort in diesem Satz ausgelassen.	auslassen
leave out	Nobody ever talks to him. He always feels **left out**. Mit ihm spricht niemand. Er fühlt sich immer übergangen.	jemanden übergehen
leave to	His mother **left** all her property **to** him. Nothing was **left to** the other children. Seine Mutter hat ihm ihr ganzes Vermögen hinterlassen. Für die anderen Kinder blieb nichts übrig.	hinterlassen, vermachen
leave up to	Why do you always **leave** the hard work **up to** me? Warum überlässt du mir immer die harte Arbeit?	überlassen

Übung 2:
Drücke die Sätze in anderen Worten aus und verwende dabei die *phrasal verbs* aus der Aufstellung.

		Deine Formulierung
1	There are always lots of words missing in his letters.	
2	The signature and the date are missing on this cheque.	
3	Your brother is making a lot of noise.	
4	Why do I have to do all the hard work? Why don't you do it?	
5	Tell him about our plan. Otherwise he will think that his opinion is not important to us.	

3 Beispiel *to let*

Phrasal verbs	Beispielsatz und Übersetzung	Deutsche Entsprechung
let down	*I hope you'll help me. Don't **let** me **down**!* Ich hoffe, du wirst mir helfen. Lass mich nicht im Stich.	im Stich lassen; herunterlassen
let in	*Let the rope down and **let** me **in**.* Lass das Seil herunter und lass mich hinein.	hineinlassen
let into	*Who **let** you **into** my room?* Wer ließ dich in mein Zimmer?	lassen in
let off	*I'll **let** you **off** this time, but don't do it again.* Ich lasse dich dieses Mal laufen, aber mache das nie wieder!	laufen lassen, nicht bestrafen
let off	*Let me **off** at the corner, please.* Lass mich bitte an der Ecke aussteigen.	aussteigen lassen
let on	*What I've just told you is a big secret, so don't **let on** that you know.* Was ich dir gerade erzählt habe, ist ein großes Geheimnis, sage darum nicht, dass du es weißt.	verraten, sich anmerken lassen
let out	*Let the dog **out**, will you?* Lass den Hund 'raus, ja?	(aus dem Haus) lassen, rauslassen

Übung 3: Beantworte die folgenden Fragen.

	Fragen	Deine Antworten
1	Who **lets** you **in** late at night when you have forgotten the door key?	
2	What do you do when a good friend of yours **lets** you **down**?	
3	Somebody has **let** the dog **in** your room, which is now in a mess. What do you do?	
4	Would you **let** somebody **off** after you have caught him stealing your money?	
5	Would you **let** somebody **off** a train if he hadn't paid the fare?	

4 Beispiel *to live*

Phrasal verbs	Beispielsatz und Übersetzung	Deutsche Entsprechung
live for	She **lives for** her children. Ihre Kinder sind alles für sie.	das Wichtigste sein, alles sein/bedeuten
live off	She's nearly 30 and she still **lives off** her parents. Sie ist fast 30 und lässt sich noch von ihren Eltern aushalten.	sich von jemandem aushalten lassen

live on	These animals **live on** leaves. Diese Tiere leben von Blättern.	leben von
live out	I don't want to **live out** my life here. Ich möchte nicht mein ganzes Leben hier verbringen.	verbringen
live through	My granddad **lived through** two world wars. Mein Großvater hat zwei Weltkriege erlebt.	erleben, durchmachen

Übung 4: Was sagt die ältere Dame? Benutze ein Wörterbuch.

	Das sagt die alte Dame	Deine Übersetzung
1	I've lived through many a famine and I've lived through many a nightmare.	
2	I've learnt to live with difficult situations.	
3	When I was 12 I had to leave home. We children couldn't live off our parents. There were too many of us.	
4	My father lived for his work and nothing else.	
5	I'm glad to be able to live out my life here in this lovely town.	

5 Beispiel *to look*

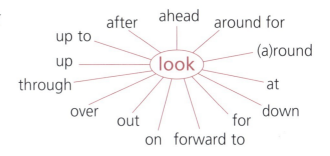

Phrasal verbs	Beispielsatz und Übersetzung	Deutsche Entsprechung
look after	Who will **look after** the cat when we're on holiday? Wer wird sich um die Katze kümmern, wenn wir im Urlaub sind?	sich kümmern um
look ahead	You live in the past. You ought to **look ahead**. Du lebst in der Vergangenheit. Du solltest lieber nach vorne schauen.	vorausschauen, nach vorne sehen

look around for	*We're looking around for a nice place to eat.* Wir sehen uns nach einem hübschen Ort zum Essen um.	sich umschauen, sich umsehen
look at	*Would you look at my car, please?* Würden Sie bitte mein Auto überprüfen?	überprüfen, ansehen; in Betracht ziehen
look down	*She's a nice girl. You really needn't look down on her.* Das ist ein nettes Mädchen. Du brauchst wirklich nicht auf sie herabzuschauen.	herabschauen
look for	*I'm looking for a new job.* Ich bin gerade auf der Suche nach einem neuen Arbeitsplatz.	suchen, auf der Suche sein
look forward to	*I'm really looking forward to seeing you soon.* Ich freue mich schon, dich bald zu sehen.	sich auf etwas freuen
look on	*She tried to help us, but all the other people just looked on.* Sie versuchte, uns zu helfen, aber alle anderen schauten nur zu.	zuschauen
look out	*Look out! There's a car coming.* Pass auf! Da kommt ein Auto.	aufpassen
look over	*I've looked over the letter. It's okay.* Ich habe den Brief durchgesehen. Er ist in Ordnung.	ansehen, mustern, durchsehen
look (a)round	*I don't want to buy anything. I'm just looking (a)round.* Ich möchte nichts kaufen. Ich sehe mich nur mal um.	sich umsehen
look through	*I saw Susan on the bus last night and she looked straight through me.* Ich sah Susan gestern Abend im Bus, aber sie sah geradewegs durch mich hindurch.	hindurchsehen
look up	*Look up the word in a dictionary.* Schlage das Wort im Wörterbuch nach.	(ein Wort) nachschlagen
look up to	*I've always looked up to Frank for his courage.* Ich habe Frank immer wegen seines Mutes bewundert.	bewundern, aufschauen

Übung 5:

Welche Übersetzung ist die richtige? Setze dein Kreuz in das richtige Kästchen.

#	Englisch		Deutsch
1	He looks down on anybody who doesn't like football.	☐	Er verachtet jeden, der nicht Fußball spielt.
		☐	Er verachtet jeden, der nicht Fußball mag.
2	I'm really looking forward to going on holiday.	☐	Ich fahre im Urlaub wirklich weg.
		☐	Ich freue mich schon richtig auf den Urlaub.
3	There might still be some mistakes in my essay. Can you look it over?	☐	Es könnten noch einige Fehler in meinem Aufsatz sein. Könnten Sie ihn durchsehen?
		☐	Es könnten noch einige Fehler in meinem Aufsatz sein. Könnten Sie die übersehen?
4	Everybody looks up to Jane.	☐	Alle bewundern Jane.
		☐	Alle schauen bei Jane gern vorbei.
		☐	Alle suchen nach Jane.
5	I don't know the meaning of this word. I'll have to look it up.	☐	Ich kenne die Bedeutung dieses Wortes nicht. Ich muss es nachschlagen.
		☐	Ich kenne die Bedeutung dieses Wortes nicht. Ich muss es suchen.
6	Why don't you play yourself instead of just looking on?	☐	Warum spielst du nicht selbst, anstatt nur zuzuschauen?
		☐	Warum spielst du nicht selbst, anstatt weiterzusuchen?
7	Could you look after Kathie while I'm at the shops?	☐	Könntest du Kathie suchen, während ich beim Einkaufen bin?
		☐	Könntest du auf Kathie aufpassen, während ich beim Einkaufen bin?
8	Don't forget to look out for snakes!	☐	Vergiss nicht, Schlangen zu besorgen.
		☐	Vergiss nicht, auf Schlangen zu achten.
9	I don't just want to look around. I'd like a new dress.	☐	Ich möchte mich nicht nur umsehen. Ich möchte ein neues Kleid.
		☐	Ich möchte mich nicht umsehen. Ich möchte ein neues Kleid.
10	Could you look at the tyres? Are they still okay?	☐	Könnten Sie die Reifen prüfen? Sind sie noch okay?
		☐	Sehen Sie die Reifen? Sind sie noch okay?

Weitere *phrasal verbs*, die mit „l" beginnen

Phrasal verbs	Beispielsatz und Übersetzung	Deutsche Entsprechung
lie down	*I must **lie down** and rest.* Ich muss mich hinlegen und ausruhen.	sich hinlegen, ausruhen
lie around	*I don't like **lying around** on the beach all day.* Ich liege nicht gern den ganzen Tag am Strand herum.	herumliegen
lie about = **lie around**	*You always leave your things **lying about**.* Du lässt deine Sachen immer herumliegen.	herumliegen
lie with	*The responsibility for this problem **lies with** you.* Die Verantwortung für dieses Problem liegt bei dir.	liegen bei
light up	*Lightning **lit up** the night sky.* Ein Blitz erhellte den Nachthimmel.	erleuchten, erhellen
light up (with)	*His face **lit up** (with joy) when he saw her.* Er begann (vor Freude) zu strahlen, als er sie sah.	strahlen, aufleuchten
light (up)	*She **lit (up)** a cigarette.* Sie zündete sich eine Zigarette an.	anzünden

Übung 6:
Ist dein Verhalten okay? Verwende ein Wörterbuch, wenn du die Sätze nicht verstehen solltest.

	Questions	Deine Antworten
1	Do you light up a cigarette when other people are still eating?	
2	Do you often leave your clothes lying about all over the house?	
3	Do you play loud music when your dad has lain down for a nap?	
4	Do you just lie around in the garden when there's plenty to do round the house?	
5	Do you think you should manage your own life, or do you think the responsibility lies with your parents?	

M

1 Beispiel *to make*

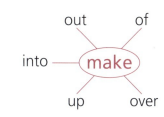

Phrasal verbs	Beispielsatz und Übersetzung	Deutsche Entsprechung
make into	*He **made** the attic **into** a nice study.* Er machte aus dem Dachboden ein hübsches Arbeitszimmer.	zu etwas machen, verändern
make out	*The writing is very small. I hardly can **make** it **out**.* Die Schrift ist sehr klein. Ich kann sie kaum entziffern.	erkennen, ausmachen, entziffern
make of	*I want to **make** something **of** my life.* Ich möchte aus meinem Leben etwas machen.	machen aus

make over	He **made over** all his money to me. Er vermachte mir sein ganzes Geld.	übereignen, vermachen
make up	It's hard to believe his story. He must have **made** it **up**. Seine Geschichte ist kaum zu glauben. Er muss sie erfunden haben.	erfinden, ausdenken
make up	I never go out without **making** myself **up** first. Ich gehe niemals weg, ohne mich zuvor geschminkt zu haben.	sich schminken, sich zurechtmachen
make up	I can **make up** a bed for you in Tom's room. Ich kann dir in Toms Zimmer ein Bett herrichten.	herrichten, zurechtmachen
make up	They **made up** after the argument and kissed each other. Sie versöhnten sich nach dem Streit und küssten sich.	versöhnen, vertragen

Übung 1: Welche Satzhälften gehören zusammen?

If you don't know a good night story for the kids	1		a	use a magnifying glass.
If you want to change the way you look	2		b	try to make one up.
If you can't make out his writing,	3		c	you can make it over to charity.
If you can't make up with each other,	4		d	you should make yourself up.
If you don't know what to do with your money,	5		e	you should separate.

Weitere *phrasal verbs*, die mit „m" beginnen

Phrasal verbs	Beispielsatz und Übersetzung	Deutsche Entsprechung
mark down	The teacher **marked** her **down** as absent. Der Lehrer notierte sie als abwesend.	notieren, aufschreiben
mark down	This jacket was really a bargain. It was **marked down** by 40%. Diese Jacke war wirklich ein Schnäppchen. Sie war um 40% reduziert.	reduzieren, herabsetzen

mark off	I've **marked off** all the things we've already bought. Ich habe alle Sachen abgehakt, die wir bereits gekauft haben.	abhaken
mark up	Cigarettes should be **marked up** by 200%. Zigaretten sollten um 200 % heraufgesetzt werden.	heraufsetzen (Preis)
mix in	Add the flour to the butter, and then **mix in** two eggs. Gib das Mehl zur Butter und rühre dann zwei Eier hinein.	hinzugeben, einrühren
mix up	It's easy to **mix** her **up** with her sister. They look so much alike. Sie kann leicht mit ihrer Schwester verwechselt werden. Sie sind sich so ähnlich.	verwechseln, vermischen
mix up	Don't **mix up** these papers. Bringe diese Papiere nicht durcheinander.	durcheinander bringen

Übung 2: Vervollständige die folgenden Sätze.

1	Fred and Tom look so much alike.	It's easy to _____
2	I don't know which things we've already packed. Why didn't you use that list I made.	You should have _____
3	We need these papers back in the given order.	So don't _____
4	We don't know which of the pupils were absent yesterday.	Nobody _____
5	These shoes are too expensive. Nobody will buy them.	So we should _____

P

1   Beispiel *to pass*

Phrasal verbs	Beispielsatz und Übersetzung	Deutsche Entsprechung
pass around	*Pass the cookies around, would you?* Lass die Plätzchen herumgehen.	herumgehen lassen
pass away	*She passed away in her sleep.* Sie verstarb im Schlaf.	sterben, versterben
pass by	*I watched the people passing by.* Ich beobachtete die Leute, die vorbeigingen.	vorbeigehen, vorbeifahren

pass down	*That skill has been **passed down** from father to son.* Der Sohn hat dieses Geschick von seinem Vater geerbt.	vererben, weitergeben
pass off	*The meeting **passed off** well.* Die Sitzung ist gut verlaufen.	verlaufen
pass on	*Read the minutes and then **pass** them **on**.* Lies das Protokoll und gebe es dann weiter.	weitergeben; fortfahren
pass on	*I'll stay at home. I don't want to **pass** my cold **on** to anyone.* Ich bleibe zu Hause. Ich möchte niemand mit meiner Erkältung anstecken.	(mit einer Krankheit) anstecken
pass out	*I always **pass out** at the sight of blood.* Ich werde beim Anblick von Blut immer ohnmächtig.	ohnmächtig werden, umfallen
pass out	*The teacher told me to **pass out** the dictionaries.* Der Lehrer sagte mir, dass ich die Wörterbücher austeilen solle.	austeilen

Übung 1:
Welche Sätze passen zusammen? Schreibe die Buchstaben in die richtige Box.

Ein Lehrer mit seiner Klasse auf einem Ausflug …	
1 Teacher: Listen, boys and girls. Here are the tickets for the train.	_____
2 Teacher: You should have stayed at home, Mary.	_____
3 Teacher: There are enough sandwiches for everybody.	_____
4 Teacher: You should look out of the window.	_____
5 Pupils: The class outing was really great.	_____

a The outing passed off well.
b Take one out and then pass the basket around.
c Would you mind passing them out?
d We're going to pass by some very interesting places.
e You might pass your flu on to everybody.

2 Beispiel *to pick*

*Tom's got a new girlfriend. He **picked** her **up** at the disco last Saturday.*

Phrasal verbs	Beispielsatz und Übersetzung	Deutsche Entsprechung
pick at	*Don't you like lamb? You're just **picking at** it.* Magst du kein Lamm? Du stocherst nur so lustlos darin herum.	(im Essen) herumstochern
pick on	*Why are you always **picking on** me?* Warum hackst du immer auf mir herum?	auf jemandem herumhacken, es auf jemand abgesehen haben

pick out	I've **picked out** a wonderful hat for you to wear with your new coat. Ich habe einen wunderschönen Hut zu deinem neuen Mantel ausgesucht.	aussuchen, auswählen (für sich)
pick up	There're lots of cigarette ends on the floor. **Pick** them **up**. Am Boden liegen viele Kippen. Hebe sie auf!	etwas vom Boden aufheben
pick up	I think I've **picked up** a cold somewhere. Ich glaube, ich habe mir irgendwo eine Erkältung geholt.	einfangen, holen (eine Krankheit)
pick up	**Pick** me **up** at 9.00. Hole mich um 9 Uhr ab.	abholen
pick up	Tom's got a new girlfriend. He **picked** her **up** at the disco last Saturday. Tom hat eine neue Freundin. Er hat sie letzten Samstag in der Disko aufgerissen.	aufreißen (ugs.)
pick up	Can you **pick up** my coat from the cleaner's? Kannst du meinen Mantel aus der Reinigung abholen?	etwas abholen
pick up	The phone's ringing. **Pick** it **up**! Das Telefon läutet. Nimm ab!	abnehmen (Telefon)

Übung 2: Übersetze nur die unterlegten Sätze.

		English	German
1	My dress has been at the cleaner's for ages.	Pick it up!	_____
2	Mary has just arrived. She's at the airport now.	Pick her up!	_____
3	There are lots of pieces of broken glass on the carpet.	Pick them up!	_____
4	Can't you hear the phone?	Pick it up!	_____

Übung 3:
Übersetze; benutze ein Wörterbuch, wenn du nicht mehr weiterweißt.

1	Why does he never stop picking on me?	_____
2	Would you mind picking up the cans on the floor?	_____
3	Leave me alone. Pick on somebody your own size.	_____
4	I would never pick up somebody on the road at night.	_____

3   Beispiel *to pull*

pull — away, apart, at, up, down, together, in, through, off, out

Stop shouting. Pull yourself together!

Phrasal verbs	Beispielsatz und Übersetzung	Deutsche Entsprechung
pull apart	The police managed to **pull** the hooligans **apart**. Der Polizei gelang es, die Hooligans auseinander zu treiben.	(Streitende) trennen, auseinander nehmen/ bringen
pull away	I jumped onto the bus just as it was **pulling away**. Ich sprang in den Bus, gerade, als er anfahren wollte.	anfahren
pull down	They **pulled down** the old houses to make room for the motorway. Sie rissen die alten Häuser ab, um Platz für die Autobahn zu schaffen.	abreißen
pull in	**Pull in** there. Fahre dort an die Seite und halte an!	(mit einem Fahrzeug) an die Seite fahren und anhalten
pull off	We **pulled off** the road to look for a quiet place for a picnic. Wir sind von der Straße abgefahren, um nach einem ruhigen Platz für ein Picknick zu suchen.	(eine Straße) verlassen, abfahren
pull out	Don't **pull out**. There's a car coming. Fahr' nicht los. Da kommt ein Auto.	ausscheren (Straße)
pull through	He's badly injured, but he'll **pull through**. Er ist schwer verletzt, aber er wird durchkommen.	durchkommen, überleben
pull together	Stop shouting! **Pull** yourself **together**! Hör auf zu schreien. Reiß dich zusammen!	sich zusammenreißen
pull up	**Pull up** a chair and sit down. Zieh dir einen Stuhl heran und setze dich!	(einen Stuhl) herziehen, heranziehen

Übung 4: Welche *phrasal verbs* passen zu welchen Definitionen?

to break (building) to pieces	1		a	to pull through
to live in spite of severe illness	2		b	to pull up a chair
to control the feelings	3		c	to pull apart
to get a chair	4		d	to pull down
to separate fighting people	5		e	to pull together

4   Beispiel *to push*

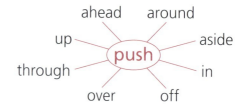

Phrasal verbs	Beispielsatz und Übersetzung	Deutsche Entsprechung
push ahead	They are pushing ahead with their plans for a new airport. Sie treiben ihre Pläne für einen neuen Flughafen voran.	etwas vorantreiben, weitermachen
push around / about	Stop pushing me around / about all the time. Hör auf, mich dauernd herumzukommandieren!	herumkommandieren, herumschieben
push aside	You should try to push it aside. Du solltest versuchen, es zu vergessen.	vergessen, verdrängen
push in	This is a queue! You can't just push in. Das ist eine Warteschlange! Du kannst dich nicht einfach hineindrängen.	hineinstoßen, hineindrängen
push off	What are doing in my garden? Push off! Was machst du in meinem Garten? Hau ab!	abhauen, verschwinden
push over	Some people were pushed over when they rushed to the exit. Einige Leute wurden umgerannt, als sie zum Ausgang eilten.	umrennen, umstoßen
push through	The law was pushed through by the government. Das Gesetz wurde von der Regierung durchgedrückt.	(ein Gesetz) durchdrücken
push up	The oil crisis has pushed up the prices. Die Ölkrise hat die Preise in die Höhe getrieben.	(Preise) in die Höhe treiben

Übung 5:
Schreibe die passenden *phrasal verbs* zu den entsprechenden Definitionen.

	Definitions	Phrasal verbs
1	To tell somebody to leave in a rude way.	
2	To increase prices rapidly.	
3	To try to forget something unpleasant.	
4	To make somebody fall to the ground.	
5	To give someone orders in a rude way.	

4 Beispiel *to put*

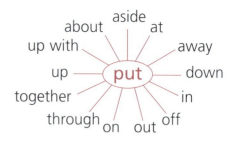

Phrasal verbs	Beispielsatz und Übersetzung	Deutsche Entsprechung
put about	*It's being put about that you're pregnant. – Well, I've certainly put a lot of weight on.* Es wird verbreitet, dass du schwanger seist. – Gewiss, ich habe ziemlich zugenommen.	verbreiten, in Umlauf bringen
put aside	*Put the paper aside and help me.* Lege die Zeitung weg und hilf mir!	beiseite legen; absehen von
put aside	*We should try to put aside some money every month.* Wir sollten versuchen, monatlich etwas Geld zu sparen.	beiseite legen, sparen
put at	*I'd put her age at 14.* Ich schätze ihr Alter auf 14.	schätzen auf
put away	*Put your books away and listen!* Räumt eure Bücher weg und passt auf!	wegräumen
put down	*Let me put down your telephone number.* Lass mich deine Telefonnummer aufschreiben.	aufschreiben, notieren
put down	*Just put me down at the gate. You needn't drive up to the house.* Lass mich am Tor aussteigen. Du brauchst nicht bis zum Haus zu fahren.	absetzen
put in	*I had a new heating system put in.* Ich ließ eine neue Heizung einbauen.	einbauen
put off	*The meeting has been put off till next month.* Die Sitzung wurde auf nächsten Monat verschoben.	verschieben, vertagen
put on	*You'd better put a sweater on. It's cold outside.* Du solltest dir einen Pullover anziehen. Es ist kalt draußen.	(ein Kleidungsstück) anziehen
put on	*Put your glasses on, if you can't read it.* Setze deine Brille auf, wenn du es nicht lesen kannst.	(eine Brille) aufsetzen
put on	*Have you put the heating on?* Hast du die Heizung angestellt?	(Heizung) anstellen, anmachen
put on	*Put a nice record on!* Lege eine schöne Platte auf.	(eine Platte) auflegen

put on	I've **put on** a lot of weight. Ich habe schwer zugenommen.	zunehmen, dicker werden
put out	I used a blanket to **put** the fire **out**. Ich benutzte eine Decke zum Löschen des Feuers.	(Feuer) löschen
put out	**Put out** your cigarette, please. Machen Sie bitte Ihre Zigarette aus.	(Zigarette) ausmachen
put out	**Put out** the light, please. Mach das Licht bitte aus!	(Licht) ausmachen
put out	Don't forget to **put** the rubbish **out**. Vergiss nicht, den Abfall hinauszubringen!	hinausbringen
put through	Can you **put** me **through** to Mrs Winters? Können Sie mich mit Mrs Winters verbinden?	(telefonisch) verbinden
put together	Do you know how to **put** this model plane **together**? Weißt du, wie man dieses Modellflugzeug zusammenbaut?	zusammensetzen, zusammenbauen
put up	Can you help me to **put up** the tent? Kannst du mir helfen, das Zelt aufzustellen?	aufstellen
put up	Where shall I **put** this picture **up**? Wo soll ich dieses Bild aufhängen?	(Bild) aufhängen
put up with	I can't **put up with** your stinginess anymore. I'm leaving you. Ich kann deinen Geiz nicht länger ertragen. Ich verlasse dich.	sich abfinden mit, ertragen

Übung 6: Führe das folgende Gespräch auf Englisch.

	A		B
1	Frage, wo du diese Bilder aufhängen sollst.	2	Sage, dass er sie irgendwo in der Küche aufhängen soll.
3	Sage, dass B das Buch weglegen und dir beim Geschirrspülen helfen soll.	4	Frage, warum A die Spülmaschine nicht benutzt.
5	Frage B, ob er den Abfall schon aus dem Haus gebracht hat.	6	Verneine dies. Sage, dass du annahmst, dass dies A bereits getan hätte.
7	Sage, dass B nicht so faul sein soll. Sage, dass er ohnehin sehr zugenommen hat.	8	Sage, dass dies nicht stimmt. Sage, dass du schon das Zelt für die Party im Garten aufgestellt hast.
9	Sage, dass B die Tassen in den Schrank räumen soll.	10	Sage, dass du das schon erledigt hast.
11	You're a good boy.	12	I know.

Weitere *phrasal verbs*, die mit "p" beginnen

Phrasal verbs	Beispielsatz und Übersetzung	Deutsche Entsprechung
piss off (vulgär)	*Why don't you just **piss off** and leave me alone?* Warum verpisst du dich nicht und lässt mich in Ruhe?	sich verpissen
pump up	*You must **pump up** the spare tyre.* Du musst den Ersatzreifen aufpumpen.	(einen Reifen) aufpumpen

Q

1 Beispiel *to quarrel*

Phrasal verbs	Beispielsatz und Übersetzung	Deutsche Entsprechung
quarrel about	*What are you quarrelling about?* Wegen was streitet ihr?	sich streiten wegen, um
quarrel with	*I don't quarrel with what you say, but with how you say it.* Ich beschwere mich nicht über das, was du sagst, sondern, wie du es sagst.	sich beschweren über

Übung 1: Wie würde man die folgenden Sätze ins Deutsche übertragen?

English	German
I wish you two would stop quarrelling with each other.	___
I'm not going to quarrel about a few pounds.	___
There's no need to quarrel with each other about that.	___

2 Beispiel *to queue*

Phrasal verbs	Beispielsatz und Übersetzung	Deutsche Entsprechung
queue (up)	You have to **queue (up)** here. The bus is going to arrive at any minute. Sie müssen sich hier anstellen. Der Bus wird gleich kommen.	sich anstellen, anstehen
queue up for	What are you **queuing up for**? Wofür stehen sie an?	sich anstellen für, anstehen für

R

1 Beispiel *to rip*

off — rip — up

*She **ripped up** the photo angrily.*

Phrasal verbs	Beispielsatz und Übersetzung	Deutsche Entsprechung
rip off	They really **ripped** us **off** at that disco. In dieser Disko wurden wir wirklich geschröpft.	ausnehmen, schröpfen
rip off	My bike has been **ripped off**. Mein Fahrrad wurde gestohlen.	klauen, stehlen
rip up	She **ripped up** the photo angrily. Sie zerriss wütend das Foto.	zerreißen

Übung 1: Welche Warnungen passen zu den folgenden Situationen?

1 Somebody might rip it off. – **2** She might rip it up. – **3** They'll rip you off.

Situations	Warnings
Don't even think about having dinner in that restaurant.	
Don't leave your bike unlocked.	
Don't show her his letter. She might get angry.	

2 Beispiel *to round*

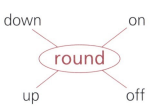

*Suddenly the rhino **rounded on** me.*

Phrasal verbs	Beispielsatz und Übersetzung	Deutsche Entsprechung
round down	You can **round** 33,08 **down** to 33. Du kannst 33,08 auf 33 abrunden.	(Zahl) abrunden
round off	We could **round off** the meal with some nice ice cream. Wir könnten das Essen mit einem schönen Eis abrunden.	abrunden (vervollständigen)
round off (AE) **round up** (BE)	**Round** $999 **off** / **up** to $1000. Runde 999 auf 1000 auf.	(Zahl) aufrunden
round on	Suddenly the rhino **rounded on** me. Plötzlich kam das Nashorn auf mich zu.	umdrehen und auf jemanden zukommen
round up	I'll **round up** some friends to help you. Ich werden ein paar Freunde zusammentrommeln, um dir zu helfen.	zusammentrommeln, auftreiben

Übung 2: Ergänze die fehlenden *phrasal verbs*.

	Deutsch	Englisch
1	Ich beende eine Rede immer mit einem Witz.	I always _____ a speech with a joke.
2	Er beendet seine Mahlzeiten immer mit einem Espresso.	He always _____ his meals with an espresso.
3	Versuche ein paar deiner Freunde zusammenzutrommeln, um ihm zu helfen.	See if you can _____ some friends to help him.
4	A: Das macht $398. B: Okay. Sie können es auf 400 aufrunden.	A: That's $398 altogether. B: Okay. You may _____ to $400.

3 Beispiel *to run*

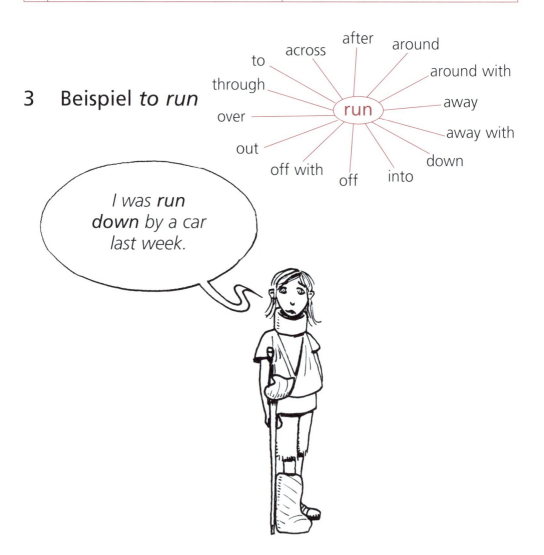

*I was **run down** by a car last week.*

Phrasal verbs	Beispielsatz und Übersetzung	Deutsche Entsprechung
run across	*I ran across an old friend last night.* Ich habe gestern Abend zufällig einen alten Freund getroffen.	(zufällig) treffen, über den Weg laufen
run after	*I ran after the thief but I couldn't get hold of him.* Ich verfolgte den Dieb, aber ich konnte ihn nicht erwischen.	hinterherlaufen, verfolgen
run around	*We were running around the whole day.* Wir liefen den ganzen Tag herum.	herumlaufen, herumtreiben
run away	*I ran away from home when I was 16.* Ich lief von zu Hause weg, als ich 16 war.	weglaufen
run down	*I was run down by a car last week.* Ich wurde letzte Woche von einem Auto überfahren.	(Fahrzeug) überfahren
run into	*I drove too fast round the corner and ran into another car.* Ich fuhr zu schnell um die Kurve und fuhr gegen ein anderes Auto.	gegen etwas fahren, stoßen auf
run off	*He had run off and left her with four kids to bring up.* Er hatte sich aus dem Staub gemacht und sie mit vier Kindern zurückgelassen.	sich aus dem Staub machen
run off with	*She ran off with all my money.* Sie machte sich mit meinem ganzen Geld aus dem Staub.	sich aus dem Staub machen, abhauen
run out	*I've run out of petrol. Can you help me?* Mir ist das Benzin ausgegangen. Können Sie mir helfen?	ausgehen, zu Ende gehen
run over	*Her cat was run over by a bus and killed.* Ihre Katze wurde von einem Bus überfahren und getötet.	überfahren
run through	*Could you just run through the first pages?* Könntest du schnell die ersten Seiten durchlesen?	(schnell) durchschauen, durchlesen, überfliegen
run through	*He soon ran through all his mother's money.* Er verpulverte bald das ganze Geld seiner Mutter.	(Geld) verpulvern, durchbringen, auf den Kopf hauen
run to	*The damage could easily run to £10,000.* Der Schaden könnte sich leicht auf 10 000 Pfund belaufen.	sich belaufen auf, umfassen

Übung 3: Beantworte die Fragen, aber sei ehrlich.

	Questions	Deine Antworten
1	Have you ever run away from home?	_____
2	Have you ever run away with your mother's money?	_____
3	Would you run after a burglar?	_____
4	Would you run around with somebody (who was) 20 years older than you?	_____
5	Have you ever run into a fence with your bike?	_____
6	Have you ever run out of ink when you were doing a test?	_____
7	Would you run through all the money, if you won the pools?	_____

Weitere *phrasal verbs*, die mit „r" beginnen

Phrasal verbs	Beispielsatz und Übersetzung	Deutsche Entsprechung
rule out	*She may have taken the money away. I can't* **rule out** *that possibility.* Sie hat das Geld vielleicht weggenommen. Ich kann diese Möglichkeit nicht ausschließen.	ausschließen
rush about / around	*I was* **rushing about / around** *all day to get everything we need for our holiday.* Ich bin den ganzen Tag herumgerannt, um alles für unseren Urlaub zu besorgen.	herumrennen, herumhetzen
rush into	*Paul has asked me to marry him, but I don't want to* **rush into** *things.* Paul hielt um meine Hand an, aber ich möchte nichts überstürzen.	überstürzen, hineinstürzen

Übung 4: Welche Sätze gehören zusammen?

The police have ruled out murder.	1		a	I've got to think about it carefully.
Don't rush me into things.	2		b	We won't need a present before Saturday.
There's no need to rush about all day.	3		c	It must have been an accident.

S

1 Beispiel *to see*

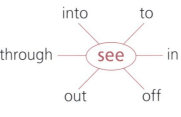

Phrasal verbs	Beispielsatz und Übersetzung	Deutsche Entsprechung
see in	I don't know what she **sees in** him. Ich weiß nicht, was sie an ihn findet.	(etwas an jemandem) finden
see into	My secretary will **see** you **into** my office. Meine Sekretärin bringt sie in mein Büro.	(an einen bestimmten Ort) bringen
see off	He's gone to the station to **see** his brother **off**. Er ist zum Bahnhof gefahren, um seinen Bruder zu verabschieden.	verabschieden
see out	**See** Mr Black **out**, would you, Peter? Begleitest du Mr Black zur Tür, Peter.	hinausbegleiten
see through	I can **see through** your lies. Ich kann deine Lügen durchschauen.	durchschauen
see to	A: This letter should get posted today. B: Okay. I'll **see to** it. A: Dieser Brief muss heute aufgegeben werden. B: Okay. Ich kümmere mich darum.	sich kümmern um

Übung 1: Beantworte die folgenden Fragen, möglichst in ganzen Sätzen.

	Questions	Deine Antworten
1	Have you ever taken visitors to the airport to see them off?	_____
2	Can you see through your sister when she pretends to be asleep?	_____
3	Which of you sees to your little sister when your parents are away?	_____
4	Do you always close the curtains at night so that no one can see in?	_____
5	Have you ever seen your grandparents out of the house?	_____

2 **Beispiel** *to send*

send — away, away for, away to, in, off, on, out

*The invitations should be **sent out** today.*

Phrasal verbs	Beispielsatz und Übersetzung	Deutsche Entsprechung
send away to	I was **sent away to** a school in Switzerland. Ich wurde auf eine Schule in der Schweiz geschickt.	wegschicken
send away for	**Send away for** your free copy. Fordern Sie Ihr kostenloses Exemplar an.	anfordern
send in	**Send in** your letters to the editor. Senden Sie ihre Briefe an den Herausgeber.	einschicken
send off	I **sent off** the parcel this morning. Ich habe das Paket heute Morgen abgeschickt.	(Brief, Paket) abschicken
send on	The letters should be **sent on** to my new address. Die Briefe sollten an meine neue Adresse geschickt werden.	nachsenden, schicken
send out	The invitations should be **sent out** today. Die Einladungen sollten heute verschickt werden.	verschicken (von Briefen)
send out	I could hear the signals the ship was **sending out**. Ich konnte die Signale hören, die das Schiff aussandte.	aussenden (von Signalen)

Übung 2: Machst du das auch? Schreibe deine Anworten auf.

	Questions	Deine Antwort
1	I often send parcels off to poor countries.	
2	I always send out lots of invitation cards when I give a party.	
3	I have the newspaper sent on when I'm on holiday.	
4	I would never send my children away to a school abroad.	

(Verwende: So do I. So have I. I don't. I haven't. So would I. I wouldn't do that either.)

3 Beispiel *to set*

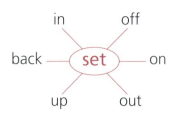

Phrasal verbs	Beispielsatz und Übersetzung	Deutsche Entsprechung
set back	The bad weather will **set** my plans **back** by weeks. Das schlechte Wetter wird meine Pläne um Wochen aufhalten.	hindern, aufhalten, verschieben
set in	I think winter seems to be **setting in** early this year. Ich glaube, dass der Winter dieses Jahr sehr früh beginnt.	einsetzen, beginnen
set off	I'd like to **set off** early in the morning. Ich möchte gern früh am Morgen losfahren.	aufbrechen, losfahren, loslaufen

set off	I **set off** the fire bell accidentally. Ich habe den Feueralarm versehentlich ausgelöst.	(Alarm) auslösen
set on	If you dare to come again, I'll **set** the dog **on** you. Wenn du es noch einmal wagst, hierher zu kommen, werde ich den Hund auf dich hetzen.	(Hunde) auf jemanden hetzen
set out	Your garden has been **set out** beautifully. Dein Garten ist sehr schön angelegt.	(Garten) anlegen, gestalten
set up	It's a lot of work **setting up** a birthday party. Es macht viel Arbeit, eine Geburtstagsparty zu organisieren.	(eine Feier) organisieren, arrangieren, ausrichten
set up	Could you **set up** the chess while I have a shower? Könntest du die Schachfiguren aufstellen, während ich dusche?	aufstellen, errichten

Übung 3:
Bringe die folgenden sechs Sätze in die richtige Reihenfolge.

I've been living on a farm far away from the city. Last week something strange happened.
1
2
3
4
5
6
I was told that they had already arrested a man. He was a horse thief.

Somebody must have set off the alarm, I thought.
Next morning I set off early to report that to the police.
I threatened to set my dog on him.
When the man saw my dog he set off down the road at great speed.
I was just setting up the Monopoly when I suddenly heard the alarm.
I ran out of the room and saw a burglar trying to get into the barn.

4 Beispiel *to settle*

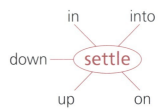

Settle down and have a cup of tea.

Phrasal verbs	Beispielsatz und Übersetzung	Deutsche Entsprechung
settle down	I want to **settle down**, get married and have kids. Ich möchte sesshaft werden, heiraten und Kinder kriegen.	sich niederlassen, sesshaft werden
settle down	*Settle down* and have a cup of tea. Mache es dir bequem und nimm eine Tasse Tee.	es sich bequem machen
settle in	I've **settled in** quickly at my new school. Ich habe mich in meiner neuen Schule sehr schnell eingelebt.	sich zurechtfinden, sich einleben

settle into	It didn't take me long to **settle into** this new routine. Ich brauchte nicht lange, um mich an diesen neuen Tagesablauf zu gewöhnen.	sich an etwas gewöhnen
settle on	We haven't **settled** yet **on** a name for the baby. Wir haben uns noch nicht auf einen Namen für das Baby geeinigt.	sich einigen, sich entscheiden
settle up	I'll **settle up** with the waitress. Ich regle das mit der Bedienung.	abrechnen, regeln

Übung 4: Wie könnte man das noch sagen?

		Sage es in deinen Worten
1	I'd like to live a quiet life.	
2	I got used to my new job quickly.	
3	She wanted a red car. I wanted a blue car. Finally we agreed on green.	
4	It's hard to get used to this new way of life.	
5	Sit down comfortably and listen.	
6	Shall I pay?	

5 Beispiel *to show*

Phrasal verbs	Beispielsatz und Übersetzung	Deutsche Entsprechung
show (a)round	*Come on, I'll show you (a)round the castle.* Komm, ich zeige dir das Schloss.	(jemandem ein Gebäude) zeigen, herumführen
show off	*Is it true or are you just showing off?* Ist das wahr oder gibst du nur an?	angeben, prahlen
show out	*My secretary will show you out.* Meine Sekretärin bringt Sie hinaus.	hinausbegleiten, hinausführen
show up	*Why did you have to show me up in front of my friends?* Warum musstest du mich vor meinen Freunden blamieren?	blamieren
show up	*I invited ten people, but nobody showed up.* Ich habe zehn Personen eingeladen, aber niemand ist erschienen.	erscheinen, sich blicken lassen
show to	*I'll show you to the room where you can wait for the doctor.* Ich bringe Sie in den Raum, wo Sie auf den Arzt warten können.	(zu einem Ort) bringen, hinführen

Übung 5:
Welche Sätze passen zusammen? Verwende ein Wörterbuch, wenn du einzelne Wörter nicht verstehen solltest.

You had better stop showing off.	1		a	He shows me up all the time.
The Pearsons are having a party on Saturday.	2		b	He showed up late for the final match.
He always tells rude jokes at parties.	3		c	We all know how clever you are.
Our coach was mad with Tom last night.	4		d	I'm not going there. All they want to do is to show off their new house.
The director will show you around the factory himself.	5		e	Yes, thank you. Can you show me to my room?
Did you have a good journey?	6		f	Thank you for coming to see me.
Mrs Miller will show you out.	7		g	He'll be here any minute.

6   Beispiel *to shut*

Phrasal verbs	Beispielsatz und Übersetzung	Deutsche Entsprechung
shut away	*He shut himself away on an island to finish his book.* Er zog sich auf eine Insel zurück, um sein Buch zu beenden.	sich zurückziehen, wegschließen
shut down	*I shut down my shop for five weeks' holiday every year.* Ich schließe meinen Laden jedes Jahr für fünf Wochen Urlaub.	(ein Geschäft) schließen, zumachen
shut down	*The firm shut down last year.* Die Firma wurde letztes Jahr geschlossen.	schließen, zumachen, stilllegen, einstellen
shut in	*It's not very kind to shut a dog in all day, is it?* Es ist nicht sehr freundlich, einen Hund den ganzen Tag einzusperren.	einschließen, einsperren
shut off	*Shut off this terrible loud music!* Stelle diese fürchterlich laute Musik ab!	abstellen
shut out	*We returned home late at night and found ourselves shut out.* Wir kamen spät in der Nacht heim und mussten feststellen, dass man uns ausgesperrt hatte.	aussperren
shut to	*You shouldn't shut your eyes to this.* Du solltest deine Augen nicht davor verschließen.	vor etwas seine Augen verschließen
shut up	*Shut up, can't you!* Halte doch endlich den Mund!	den Mund halten
shut up	*The poor dog was shut up the whole day in the cellar.* Der arme Hund war den ganzen Tag im Keller eingesperrt.	einsperren, einschließen

Übung 6:

Das macht dein schrecklicher Nachbar. Versuche auf Englisch zu reagieren und verwende dabei die *phrasal verbs* aus der Aufstellung.

	This is what my horrible neighbour does.	Deine Entgegnung auf Englisch
1	While he is out he always leaves his dog in the house. He spends most of his time in the local pub.	

2	He always listens to loud music even on Sundays without a break.	
3	He never lets the dog in the house during the night – even with temperatures below freezing point.	
4	He always uses rude words to tell somebody to stop talking.	
5	He is sometimes very cruel to his animals.	

7 **Beispiel** *to sign*

*He **signed up** for the army.*

Phrasal verbs	Beispielsatz und Übersetzung	Deutsche Entsprechung
sign for	*Would you please **sign for** this parcel?* Würden Sie bitte den Empfang des Pakets bestätigen?	den Empfang durch Unterschrift bestätigen
sign in	*When you enter this firm you have to **sign in**.* Wenn man diese Firma betritt, muss man sich eintragen.	sich (in eine Besucherliste) eintragen
sign out	*As you leave you have to **sign out**.* Beim Verlassen muss man sich wieder austragen.	sich (aus einer Besucherliste) austragen
sign off	*I **signed off** and went into business by myself.* Ich kündigte und machte mich selbstständig.	(eine Firma) verlassen, kündigen
sign over	*The house was **signed over** to me last year.* Das Haus wurde mir letztes Jahr überschrieben.	(Immobilie) überschreiben, übertragen (Rechte)
sign up sign on	*He **signed up** for the army.* Er verpflichtete sich bei der Armee.	sich verpflichten (Armee), einschreiben

Übung 7: Welche Bedeutung ist die richtige?

1 You have to sign for the money.

a =	You prove that you need the money.
b =	You prove that you have received the money.
c =	You prove that you want some money.
d =	You prove that you have lost the money.

2 Everybody has to sign in when entering our office building.

a =	You have to show that you are able to write.
b =	You have to ask for a written permission.
c =	You have to write your name into a book.
d =	You have to leave your signature for the police.

3 You have to sign on this French course.

a	= You have to put your name on a list because you want to do this course.
b	= You can't afford the fees.
c	= You have to prove that you can't speak French.

4 You have to sign the house over to your daughter.

a	= Your daughter has to sign an official document.
b	= You have to prove that this is your house.
c	= You have to pay the money the house is worth.
d	= You have to sign an official document.

8   Beispiel *to sit*

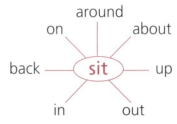

Phrasal verbs	Beispielsatz und Übersetzung	Deutsche Entsprechung
sit around / about	*I got tired of sitting around / about the park, so I went home.* Ich hatte es satt, im Park herumzusitzen, deshalb ging ich nach Hause.	herumsitzen
sit back	*Sit back and relax.* Mach es dir bequem und entspanne dich.	es sich bequem machen, sich zurücklehnen
sit down	*Why don't you sit down and tell me about it?* Warum setzt du dich nicht und erzählst mir davon?	sich setzen
sit in	*Why don't you sit in this armchair? It's more comfortable.* Warum setzt du dich nicht in diesen Sessel? Er ist bequemer.	sich in einen Sessel setzen
sit on	*They asked me to sit on the committee. They were very conservative and any new idea was immediately sat on.* Sie baten mich in diesem Ausschuss zu sitzen. Sie waren sehr konservativ und jede neue Idee wurde sofort unterdrückt.	sitzen in (Ausschuss); unterdrücken
sit out	*Tom sat out a whole concert although he was bored to tears.* Tom hielt das gesamte Konzert durch, obwohl er sich zu Tode langweilte.	durchhalten
sit up	*She sat up in bed staring at me.* Sie setzte sich auf im Bett und starrte mich an.	sich aufsetzen, gerade sitzen

Übung 8: Findest du die fehlenden Wörter?

My friend Bill

My friend Bill is a real couch-potato. He likes sitting (**1**) watching TV all day. He always sits (**2**) and lets me do all the work. So I hardly have time to sit (**3**) beside him and talk to him. Sometimes I succeed to sit (**4**) a whole sitcom with him. Last night he fell asleep in front of the telly. He sat (**5**) and rubbed his eyes and then he went to bed. He's a real sweet, isn't he?

(**1**) _____
(**2**) _____
(**3**) _____
(**4**) _____
(**5**) _____

9 Beispiel *to slip*

Phrasal verbs	Beispielsatz und Übersetzung	Deutsche Entsprechung
slip away	I'd like to **slip away** before the end of the party. Ich würde mich gerne vor dem Ende der Party aus den Staub machen.	sich fortschleichen
slip into	He came in, **slipped into** his new jacket and left the house again. Er kam, schlüpfte in seine neue Jacke und verließ wieder das Haus.	hineinschlüpfen (Kleidung)
slip on	It was very cold outside. So I **slipped** a coat **on**. Es war sehr kalt draußen. Deswegen zog ich einen Mantel an.	überstreifen, anziehen
slip off	She **slipped off** her coat and sat down. Sie zog schnell ihren Mantel aus und setzte sich.	ausziehen, abstreifen
slip out of	Her car key **slipped out** of her handbag. Ihr Autoschlüssel rutschte aus ihrer Handtasche.	herausrutschen

Übung 9:
Finde die passende deutsche Entsprechung zu folgenden Aussagen.

1 Let me just slip into something more comfortable.

a	= Ich würde es gern etwas bequemer haben.
b	= Lass es uns gemütlich machen.
c	= Schauen wir uns nach etwas Bequemerem um.
d	= Ich würde gern etwas Bequemeres anziehen.

2 I slipped off my jacket and went upstairs.

a	= Ich rutschte auf meiner Jacke aus und ging nach oben.
b	= Ich zog schnell meine Jacke aus und ging nach oben.
c	= Ich zog mir oft die Jacke aus und ging nach oben.

3 I didn't want to say that – it just slipped out.

a	= Ich wollte das nicht sagen – es ist mir aus der Hand gerutscht.
b	= Ich wollte das nicht sagen, aber ich bin ausgerutscht.
c	= Ich wollte das nicht sagen – es ist mir nur so herausgerutscht.
d	= Ich wollte das nicht sagen – ich bin gerade ausgerutscht.

10 Beispiel *to stay*

*Sue left school at sixteen but Sally **stayed on** to do A-levels.*

Phrasal verbs	Beispielsatz und Übersetzung	Deutsche Entsprechung
stay at	I **stayed** the night **at** a friend's house. Ich verbrachte die Nacht bei einem Freund.	bei (jemandem) bleiben
stay away	She **stayed away** from the meetings at her youth club and nobody knew the reason. Sie blieb den Treffen in ihrem Jugendklub fern und niemand kannte den Grund.	wegbleiben, fernbleiben
stay with	We've got some friends **staying with** us this weekend. Einige Freunde verbringen das Wochenende bei uns.	verbringen, (vorübergehend) wohnen bei
stay back **stay behind**	The police told us to **stay back / behind**. Die Polizei wies uns an zurückzubleiben.	zurückbleiben
stay in	The whole class will have to **stay in** after school. Die ganze Klasse muss nach dem Unterricht hier bleiben.	bleiben

stay on	Sue left school at sixteen but Sally **stayed on** to do A-levels. Sue verließ die Schule mit sechzehn, aber Sally blieb, um das Abitur zu machen.	(da)bleiben
stay out	Don't **stay out** too long. Bleibe nicht zu lange weg.	wegbleiben
stay off	**Stay off** the road. Use the path. Halte dich von der Straße fern. Benutzte den Weg.	fern halten, nicht benutzen
stay up	I **stayed up** to watch the late-night show. Ich blieb auf, um die Mitternachtsshow zu sehen.	aufbleiben

Übung 10: Ordne die Personen den Sätzen zu.

	Who said what?	
a		"You stay away from my daughter, will you!"
b		"You have to stay behind for half an hour after school."
c		"Why don't we stay in and watch television?"
d		"I don't want you staying out that long."
e		"I stayed up late to watch that film."
f		"Stay off the motorway. It's too crowded at this time of the day."
g		"Stay with me for a few more minutes, will you?"
h		"I stayed at that hotel for two weeks. It was great."
i		"Stay back. The fire might spread suddenly."
j		"Stay for dinner, we'd love to have you."

1	2	3	4	5
a lover	a holiday maker	an angry mother	an angry headmaster	a policeman

6	7	8	9	10
a fireman	a couch-potato	good neighbours	a movie fan	an angry father

11 Beispiel *to step*

*If the fighting goes on, the police will have to **step in**.*

Phrasal verbs	Beispielsatz und Übersetzung	Deutsche Entsprechung
step aside	We **stepped aside** to let the blind man through. Wir gingen zur Seite, um den blinden Mann vorbeizulassen.	zur Seite treten
step back	***Step back!*** *You're going to fall down the cliff.* Tritt zurück! Du fällst gleich die Klippe hinunter!	zurücktreten
step forward	*Witnesses of the accident are asked to **step forward**.* Zeugen des Unfalls werden gebeten sich zu melden.	sich melden
step down = **stand down**	*If you're going to apply for the job, I'll **step down**. I think you can do it better.* Wenn du dich um den Job bewirbst, verzichte ich. Ich glaube, dass du ihn besser machen kannst.	verzichten
step in	*If the fighting goes on, the police will have to **step in**.* Wenn die Auseinandersetzungen anhalten, wird die Polizei einschreiten müssen.	einschreiten, eingreifen

step off	As the Queen **stepped off** her coach, the crowd cheered. Als die Königin aus der Kutsche stieg, jubelte die Menge.	aussteigen (aus einem Fahrzeug)
step out / outside	He's not in at the moment. He's just **stepped out / outside** for some fresh air. Er ist momentan nicht hier. Er ist kurz hinausgegangen, um etwas frische Luft zu schnappen.	hinausgehen
step up	We have to **step up** productivity. Wir müssen die Produktivität steigern.	steigern, erhöhen

Übung 11:

Schreibe die angegebenen *phrasal verbs* in die richtigen Lücken.

1	_____ and let the doctor through.	a	stepped up
2	She has just _____ but she'll be back soon.	b	step back
3	All airlines have _____ security checks.	c	step on
4	_____ and you'll have a better view of the house.	d	step off
5	Be careful when you _____ the lorry.	e	stepped in
6	A policeman _____ and stopped the fight.	f	stepped out
7	Mind where you're going. You might _____ some broken glass.	g	step aside

Weitere *phrasal verbs*, die mit "s" beginnen

Phrasal verbs	Beispielsatz und Übersetzung	Deutsche Entsprechung
speak for	I can't **speak for** the rest of the family, but I'm against the idea. Ich kann nicht für die ganze Familie sprechen, aber ich bin gegen die Idee.	sprechen für
speak out / up	**Speak out/up**, please, we can't hear you. Sprich bitte lauter, wir können dich nicht hören.	lauter sprechen
speak up for	The poor boy has no one to **speak up for** him. Der arme Junge hat niemand, der sich für ihn einsetzt.	sich für jemanden einsetzen, aussprechen

T

1 Beispiel *to take*

*Mike really **takes after** his father.*

Phrasal verbs	Beispielsatz und Übersetzung	Deutsche Entsprechung
take after	Mike really **takes after** his father. Mike ist seinem Vater wirklich ähnlich.	jemandem ähnlich sein
take apart	I **took** the vacuum cleaner **apart** to see what was wrong with it. Ich nahm den Staubsauger auseinander, um herauszufinden, was kaputt war.	(ein Gerät) auseinander nehmen; auseinander nehmen (kritisieren)
take away	My neighbour was **taken away** in handcuffs. Mein Nachbar wurde in Handschellen abgeführt.	jemanden abführen

take back	*The jacket really doesn't fit. **Take** it **back**.* Die Jacke passt wirklich nicht. Bringe sie zurück.	zurückbringen
take down	*Everything you say will be **taken down**.* Alles, was Sie sagen, wird aufgeschrieben.	aufschreiben, notieren, schriftlich festhalten
take in	***Take** the washing **in**, it's raining!* Bringe die Wäsche ins Haus, es regnet!	ins Haus bringen
take off	***Take** your boots **off**, will you?* Ziehe sofort deine Schuhe aus.	(ein Kleidungsstück) ausziehen
take off	*The plane **takes off** in a minute.* Das Flugzeug startet in einer Minute.	(Flugzeug) starten
take off	*I **took** a day **off** to see the doctor.* Ich nahm mir einen Tag frei, um zum Arzt zu gehen.	(einen Tag) freinehmen
take on	*The word "justice" is **taking on** a new meaning.* Das Wort „Gerechtigkeit" nimmt eine neue Bedeutung an.	annehmen
take on	*They **took** her **on** because her English was excellent.* Sie wurde eingestellt, weil ihr Englisch ausgezeichnet war.	einstellen
take out	*I'm **taking** Mary **out** on Saturday.* Ich führe Mary am Samstag aus.	jemanden ausführen, mit jemandem ausgehen
take over	*I'm soon going to **take over** the business.* Ich werde die Geschäfte bald übernehmen.	(Geschäft, Verantwortung) übernehmen
take round	*Let me **take** you **round** the city. There's so much to see.* Lass mich dir die Stadt zeigen. Es gibt so viel zu sehen.	jemandem etwas zeigen, jemanden herumführen
take to	*Tim's girlfriend is lovely. I **took to** her straight away.* Tims Freundin ist Klasse. Ich fühlte mich sofort zu ihr hingezogen.	sich hingezogen fühlen, sich erwärmen für
take up	*I've never been skiing, but I think I'd like to **take** it **up**.* Ich bin noch nie Ski gelaufen, aber ich denke, es würde mir Spaß machen, damit zu beginnen.	etwas anfangen, mit etwas beginnen

Übung 1:
Armer Simon! Warum ist er so traurig? Kannst du das jemandem übersetzen, der kein Englisch kann?

1 Mum should have taken all the sweets away from me.

2 Mum shouldn't have taken me to school by car every day.

3 I have to see the dentist tomorrow to have my last tooth taken out.

4 I bought a new jacket last night. The shop will take it back if it doesn't fit. It won't fit anyway.

5 I can't take my boots off mystelf. I need some help.

6 I should have taken up jogging. I wouldn't have put on so much weight.

7 I haven't been taken out for ages. Nobody likes me.

8 The books are due back tomorrow. I should take them back to the library, but I'm too tired.

1 _____
2 _____
3 _____
4 _____
5 _____
6 _____
7 _____
8 _____

2 Beispiel *to talk*

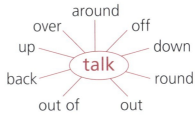

Phrasal verbs	Beispielsatz und Übersetzung	Deutsche Entsprechung
talk back	Don't **talk back** to me all the time. Gib mir nicht dauernd so freche Antworten.	jemandem frech antworten
talk down	I don't like it when you are **talking down** to me. Ich mag es nicht, wenn du von oben herab zu mir sprichst.	von oben herab sprechen, herablassend sprechen
talk out	I think the whole problem has now been **talked out.** Ich denke, dass das ganze Problem nun ausführlich besprochen wurde.	etwas ausführlich besprechen
talk out of	Jim wants to go abroad – can't you **talk** him **out of** such a foolish idea? Jim will ins Ausland. Kannst du ihm diese blöde Idee nicht ausreden?	jemandem etwas ausreden

talk over	I'd like to **talk over** this contract again. Ich würde diesen Vertrag gern nochmals besprechen.	etwas (ausführlich) besprechen
talk (a)round	I was able to **talk** her **round** and she signed the contract. Ich konnte sie überreden und sie unterschrieb den Vertrag.	jemanden überreden
talk round	He never comes to the point. He always **talks round** the problems. Er kommt niemals auf den Punkt. Er redet immer um den Brei herum.	um etwas herumreden
talk up	You'll have to **talk up** a **bit**. Du musst etwas lauter reden.	lauter reden, sprechen

Übung 2: Wie würdest du die folgenden Regeln für Lehrkräfte im Deutschen ausdrücken?

	Englisch	Deutsch
1	Don't contact the parents too early. Always talk things over with the kids first.	
2	Don't let the kids talk back in a rude way.	
3	Never talk down to the kids.	
4	Don't talk round when you explain something.	
5	Don't try to talk them round but convince them of your point.	

3 Beispiel *to tear*

Phrasal verbs	Beispielsatz und Übersetzung	Deutsche Entsprechung
tear apart	I'll **tear** her **apart**, when she comes home. Ich reiße sie in Stücke, wenn sie nach Hause kommt.	jemanden oder etwas in Stücke reißen, zerreißen
tear down	The old farms were **torn down** and replaced by a supermarket. Die alten Bauernhöfe wurde abgerissen und durch einen Supermarkt ersetzt.	(ein Gebäude) abreißen, niederreißen
tear into	**Tear** this paper **into** four pieces. Zerreiße dieses Papier in vier Stücke.	zerreißen; zerfleischen
tear off	His arm was **torn off** by the bomb. Die Bombe riss seinen Arm ab.	etwas ab-/wegreißen
tear out	I've **torn out** this picture from the newspaper. Ich habe dieses Bild aus der Zeitung herausgerissen.	etwas herausreißen
tear up	Our road has been **torn up** again. Unsere Straße wurde wieder aufgerissen.	(eine Straße) aufreißen

Übung 3:
Schreibe die passenden Urheber in die richtigen Kästchen.

1	Who's torn up the newspaper? I haven't read it yet.	
2	Who's torn out the telephone wires? I can't phone the police.	
3	I like tearing my pancake to pieces.	
4	Who has torn up our street again?	

The thieves. – The workmen from the telephone company. – The dog. – A little boy.

4   Beispiel *to think*

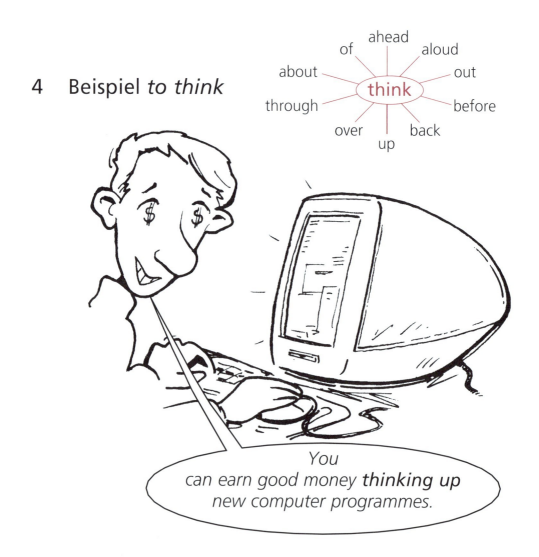

You can earn good money **thinking up** new computer programmes.

Phrasal verbs	Beispielsatz und Übersetzung	Deutsche Entsprechung
think about	*Can we go to the zoo tomorrow. – I don't know. I'll think about it.* Können wir morgen in den Zoo gehen. Ich weiß es nicht. Ich muss mir das überlegen.	sich etwas überlegen, nachdenken über
think ahead	*He can't think two minutes ahead.* Er kann keine zwei Minuten vorausdenken.	vorausdenken
think aloud	*I wasn't talking to you, I was just thinking aloud.* Ich habe nicht mit dir gesprochen. Ich habe nur laut gedacht.	laut denken
think out / through	*The plan has been really well thought out.* Der Plan ist wirklich gut durchdacht.	etwas durchdenken; ausdenken
think back to	*This photo makes me think back to my childhood.* Dieses Foto lässt mich an meine Kindheit zurückdenken.	zurückerinnern an, zurückdenken an
think of	*I've never thought of becoming an astronaut.* Ich habe nie in Betracht gezogen, Astronaut zu werden.	in Erwägung / Betracht ziehen, denken an
think over	*Think it over and let me know your answer.* Denk darüber nach und lass mich deine Antwort wissen.	überlegen, überdenken
think up	*You can earn good money thinking up new computer programmes.* Du kannst viel Geld verdienen, wenn du dir neue Computer Programme ausdenkst.	ausdenken, erfinden

Übung 4: Ergänze die fehlenden Begleiter.

1 Have you ever	thought		anyone else, but yourself?
2 Sorry, I didn't listen. I was	thinking		something else.
3 What are you	thinking		?
4 Will you	think		me after I have left?
5	Thinking		can help you solve a problem.
6 The plan has to be	thought		carefully.
7 There's no use	thinking		this silly idea. It's rubbish.
8	Thinking		new ways of storing information can make you rich.

5   Beispiel *to throw*

*He's got a great job with a company car **thrown in**.*

Phrasal verbs	Beispielsatz und Übersetzung	Deutsche Entsprechung
throw about/ around	Stop throwing stones about / around, you boys. Hört auf Steine herumzuwerfen, ihr Kerle.	herumwerfen, mit etwas um sich werfen
throw away	Throw the old racket away, we should get a now one. Wirf den alten Tennisschläger weg, wir sollten einen neuen besorgen.	etwas wegwerfen
throw back	This illness will throw me back in my work badly. Diese Krankheit wird mich in meiner Arbeit stark zurückwerfen.	zurückwerfen
throw down	He threw down some money and left. Er warf etwas Geld hin und ging.	hinwerfen
throw in	He's got a great job with a company car thrown in. Er hat einen tollen Job und einen Dienstwagen dazubekommen.	(gratis) dazugeben
throw in	She didn't really join in the conversation, she just threw in a remark now and then. Sie beteiligte sich nicht richtig an der Unterhaltung, sie warf nur hin und wieder eine Bemerkung ein.	einwerfen, einstreuen
throw off	I threw off my jacket and jumped into the river to save the kid. Ich zog schnell die Jacke aus und sprang in den Fluss, um das Kind zu retten.	ablegen, von sich werfen
throw out	If you don't pay the rent I'll throw you out. Wenn du die Miete nicht bezahlst, werfe ich dich raus.	hinauswerfen, kündigen
throw up	He was fed up of the company and so he threw up his job. Er hatte genug von der Firma und warf darum seinen Job hin.	aufgeben, hinwerfen
throw up = to vomit	He always has to throw up when crossing the Channel by ferry. Er muss sich immer übergeben, wenn er den Ärmelkanal mit der Fähre überquert.	sich übergeben, brechen (umgangssprachlich)

Übung 5: Suche ein passendes Ende für die folgenden Sätze.

1 The fish smells bad. You'd better _____

2 The newspapers are recyclable. So don't _____

3 He doesn't get on well with his colleagues and he's always late. You'd better _____

4 They were late already but the illness of Jake _____

5 School is boring some time but you shouldn't _____

6 You didn't want to join our conversation so please stop _____

6 Beispiel *to turn*

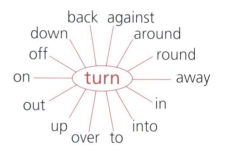

Please **turn** the radio **down**.

Phrasal verbs	Beispielsatz und Übersetzung	Deutsche Entsprechung
turn against	When Tom finished with Sue her friends **turned against** him. Als Tom mit Sue Schluss machte, wendeten sich ihre Freunde gegen ihn.	sich gegen jemanden wenden
turn around / round	She **turned around / round** and began to cry. Sie drehte sich um und begann zu weinen.	sich umdrehen, sich abwenden
turn away	Patients had to be **turned away** because of staff shortage. Patienten mussten wegen Personalmangel abgewiesen werden.	abweisen, wegschicken
turn back	You can't **turn back** the clock. The world has changed. Du kannst die Uhr nicht zurückdrehen. Die Welt hat sich verändert.	(Uhr) zurückdrehen
turn back	We were **turned back** at the border. Wir wurden an der Grenze zurückgeschickt.	jemanden zurückschicken, zurückweisen
turn down	Please **turn** the radio **down**. Stelle das Radio leiser!	(Radio) leiser stellen, niedriger stellen
turn down	I applied for the job. But they **turned** me **down** again. Ich bewarb mich um die Stelle, aber sie haben mich erneut abgewiesen.	jemanden abweisen, ablehnen
turn in	I've finished my essay, but I haven't **turned** it **in** yet. Ich habe meinen Aufsatz beendet, aber ich habe ihn noch nicht abgegeben.	abgeben
turn into	I **turned into** the High Street. Ich bog in die High Street ein.	einbiegen (in eine Straße)
turn into	A caterpillar **turns into** a butterfly. Eine Raupe verwandelt sich in einen Schmetterling.	sich verwandeln in
turn off	**Turn** the TV **off** now. Jetzt schalte den Fernseher aus!	(Radio, Fernseher) ausschalten
turn on	Please **turn** the lights **on**. Bitte schalte das Licht an!	(Licht) anschalten
turn out	Don't forget to **turn out** all the lights when leaving the office. Vergiss nicht, alle Lichter auszuschalten, wenn du das Büro verlässt.	(Licht) ausschalten

turn over	My car **turned over** three times. Mein Auto überschlug sich dreimal.	sich überschlagen
turn to	I know there's always somebody I can **turn to** in times of trouble. Ich weiß, dass es immer jemanden gibt, an den ich mich wenden kann, wenn ich Sorgen habe.	sich an jemanden wenden (um Hilfe)
turn up	Could you **turn** the radio **up**? Könntest du das Radio lauter stellen.	lauter stellen

Übung 6: Was bedeuten die folgenden Anweisungen?

1 "Turn the stereo down!"

a	Du sollst die Stereoanlage ausschalten.
b	Du sollst die Stereoanlage leiser stellen.
c	Du sollst die Stereoanlage zertrümmern.

2 "You must turn in your report on Friday at the latest."

a	Du sollst den Bericht nicht vor Freitag abgeben.
b	Du sollst den Bericht abgeben, aber am Freitag ist es bereits zu spät.
c	Du sollst den Bericht bis spätestens Freitag abgeben.

3 "I'm cold. Turn the heating on, will you?"

a	Du sollst die Heizung anstellen.
b	Du sollst dich auf die Heizung setzen.
c	Du sollst dich vor die Heizung setzen.

4 "I can hardly hear the music. Can you turn it up a little?"

a	Du sollst die Musik abstellen.
b	Du sollst die Musik lauter stellen.
c	Du sollst die Musik etwas lauter stellen.

5 "Don't try to turn me into a teacher. I'm not made for it."

a	Du sollst nicht versuchen, aus dem Sprecher einen Lehrer zu machen.
b	Du sollst versuchen, den Sprecher zu überreden, Lehrer zu werden.
c	Du sollst nicht versuchen, den Lehrer zu spielen.

W

1 Beispiel *to walk*

I walked into a pool of mud.

Phrasal verbs	Beispielsatz und Übersetzung	Deutsche Entsprechung
walk about / around	*I walked about the pedestrian area.* Ich lief in der Fußgängerzone herum.	herumlaufen
walk away / off	*You just can't walk away / off like this.* Du kannst doch nicht einfach so weggehen.	weggehen, jemanden verlassen
walk in	*I bought a ticket and walked in.* Ich kaufte eine Karte und ging hinein.	hineingehen, hereinkommen
walk into	*I walked into a pool of mud.* Ich trat in ein Schlammloch.	betreten, treten in
walk on	*I have to do up my shoelace. You can walk on.* Ich muss mir die Schnürsenkel binden. Du kannst weitergehen.	weitergehen
walk up to	*She walked up to him and slapped him.* Sie ging auf ihn zu und gab ihm eine Ohrfeige.	auf jemanden zugehen

Übung 1:

Susan und Mary sind Schwestern, aber sie sind sehr verschieden. Mary will immer genau das Gegenteil. Schreibe die passenden Sätze auf die Leerzeilen.

	Susan	Mary
1	You just can't walk away like this and leave me alone.	
2	Have you finished your meal? Let's walk on then.	
3	Shall we walk about the park?	
4	Why don't you walk up to him and tell him the truth?	
5	It's a gorgeous shop. Shall we walk in?	
6	Take your shoes off. You've just walked into something.	

a	No, it's far too expensive. We can't afford this kind of clothes.
b	No, I'll leave them on.
c	I'd rather you do it.
d	You should have thought about what you were saying.
e	No, I'd rather stay here for another couple of minutes.
f	No, I'd rather sit down somewhere and have a cup of tea.

2 Beispiel *to work*

*I **worked off** my anger by chopping some wood.*

Phrasal verbs	Beispielsatz und Übersetzung	Deutsche Entsprechung
work in	*He **worked** some nice jokes **in** his lecture.* Er baute einige hübsche Scherze in seinen Vortrag ein.	einbauen, hineinbringen
work off	*You have five years to **work off** the debts.* Du hast fünf Jahre Zeit, die Schulden abzuarbeiten.	(Schulden) abarbeiten, abtragen
work off	*I **worked off** my anger by chopping some wood.* Ich reagierte mich ab, indem ich Holz hackte.	(Wut) abreagieren
work on	*I'm **working on** a new book.* Ich arbeite gerade an einem neuen Buch.	arbeiten an
work out	*I'll try to **work out** what it will all cost.* Ich versuche auszurechnen, wie viel das alles kosten wird.	ausrechnen / herausfinden

work through	I've been **working through** this pile of letters all day. Ich arbeite mich schon den ganzen Tag durch diesen Stoß von Briefen.	durcharbeiten
work up	The audience had **worked** themselves **up** into a frenzy when the group appeared. Die Zuschauer hatten sich in Raserei gesteigert, als die Gruppe erschien.	sich hineinsteigern
work up	He's a skilled worker. He'll **work** his way **up**. Er ist ein geschickter Arbeiter. Er wird sich hocharbeiten.	hocharbeiten, hinarbeiten auf

Übung 2: Ergänze die fehlenden Begleiter.

1 I spent the whole weekend working		my book.
2 I was trying to work		my frustration.
3 The problem is very difficult. It will take us a while to work it		.
4 Clean your hands carefully after you have worked		the grease.
5 I'll never manage to work		all my debts.

3 Beispiel *to write*

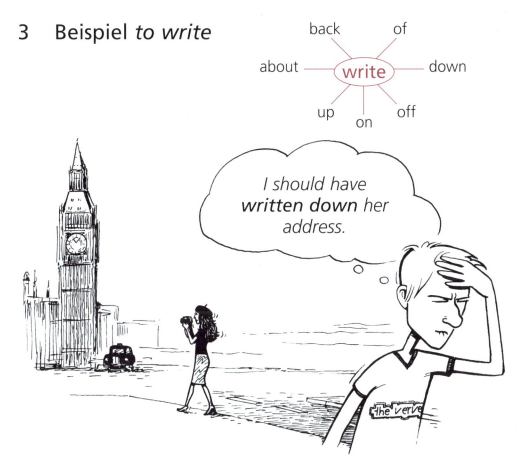

Phrasal verbs	Beispielsatz und Übersetzung	Deutsche Entsprechung
write about/ of/on	I could **write** a book **about** my teachers. Ich könnte ein Buch über meine Lehrer schreiben.	schreiben über
write away	Before you order this computer you should better **write away** for some information first. Bevor du diesen Computer kaufst, solltest du lieber zuerst Informationen (schriftlich) anfordern.	(schriftlich) anfordern
write back	I've sent her five letters, but she's never **written back**. Ich habe ihr fünf Briefe geschickt, aber sie hat sie nicht beantwortet.	zurückschreiben
write down	I should have **written down** her address. Ich hätte mir ihre Adresse notieren sollen.	aufschreiben, zu Papier bringen, notieren

write off	The library **writes off** lots of books every year. Die Bibliothek schreibt jedes Jahr viele Bücher ab.	abschreiben (von Verlusten)
write out	It will take you another week to **write out** the essay. Du wirst noch eine Woche brauchen, um den Aufsatz auszuarbeiten.	ausschreiben (Scheck, Rezept); ausarbeiten
write up	I saw your name **written up** on the poster. Ich sah deinen Namen auf dem Poster.	schreiben auf (ein Plakat)

Übung 3: Übersetze die folgenden letzten Zeilen eines Briefes.

a	Write back soon!
b	Have you already written me off?
c	I forgot to write down your telephone number. Ring me up!
d	Can't you think of anything to write about?

a _____

b _____

c _____

d _____

Lösungen zu den Übungen

In einigen Fällen sind es nur Lösungsvorschläge. Auch andere Lösungen wären durchaus möglich.

S. 6	**1** about, **2** in, **3** for, **4** round, **5** out, **6** to, **7** for, **8** after, **9** out, **10** of
S. 7	**1** Wenn du bei diesem Wetter mit den Auto fährst, forderst du dein Schicksal heraus. **2** Frage ihn nach seinem Namen (hier steht im Englischen kein *for*). **3** Bittet er wirklich um ein so altes Auto?
S. 8	**1**/2 – **2**/1 – **3**/1 – **4**/2
S. 10	**1** broke down, **2** broke up with, **3** broke into, **4** broke down, **5** broke out of, **6** broken off
S. 12	**A**6, **B**5, **C**8, **D**4, **E**10, **F**7, **G**2, **H**9, **I**1, **J**3
S. 13	**1** up, **2** back, **3** round, **4** down, **5** in, **6** about, **7** along, **8** up, **9** about, **10** round
S. 15	**1** If you don't brush up your English, nobody will understand what you say. **2** Be careful. You might bump into the wall. **3** Back up your files. Otherwise you might lose them. **4** Stop smoking immediately. Or do you want to blow the house up? **5** The meteorite burned up in the atmosphere. **6** Don't blow up that balloon too much. It might burst.
S. 17	**1** Can I call you back? **2** Call me up as soon as possible. **3** They've just called off the tennis match. **4** We can call on Anne after dinner. **5** Call for me at 5 o'clock, please.
S. 19	**1**/2- **2**/2 – **3**/1 – **4**/1 – **5**/2
S. 20	**1** – to cut down my essay a bit. **2** – to learn more to catch up with the other pupils. **3** – to cheer up. **4** – I could count on him. **5** – to clear up my desk.
S. 22	**1** drop in on, **2** drops in, **3** dropped out, **4** drops off, **5** drop … off, **6** drop …off
S. 25	**1** Do up your blouse. **2** You needn't dress up like that. **3** You can dress up as a (clown)./Why don't you dress up as a (clown)? **4** I can give you a lift and drop you off at the airport. The airport is on my way home anyway. **5** Deal out eight cards for each player. **6** I'm dealing with this problem. **7** Your letter's full of mistakes. You'd better do it over. **8** You are dropping off. **9** You should drop in on your parents. / Why don't you drop in on your parents? **10** I wouldn't drop out of school if I were you. **11** Let us drink to Grandma's birthday. **12** I must dash off now.
S. 27	**1** If you don't stop stealing things, you'll end up in prison. **2** If you don't stop smoking, you'll end up with lung cancer. **3** If you don't stop looking at other women, your marriage will end up in divorce. **4** If you don't stop working that hard, you'll end up in hospital.
S. 28	**a**3, **b**5, **c**4, **d**2, **e**1
S. 30	**1** fell over, **2** falling apart, **3** fell behind, **4** fell on, **5** fallen off, **6** fell through, **7** falling out

S. 32	**1** Try to find out what's wrong with this car. **2** Why do I have to fill in this form? **3** Nobody has been able to figure out the problem. **4** I've got to face up to reality and sell the car. **5** Fill her up, please. **6** I feel like a cup of coffee. **7** We should fix up something for the next week.
S. 35	**1** get up – **2** get … up – **3** get on – **4** get … back – **5** get out – **6** get together – **7** got away – **8** gets … into
S. 37	**1** Ich hatte Glück. Ich hatte einen schweren Unfall, aber ich lebe noch. Nun hat sich mein Leben sehr verändert. **2** Die Ärzte sollten niemals jemanden aufgeben. **3** Wenn du meinst, du hast recht, gib niemals nach. **4** Opfere einen Teil deiner Freizeit, um Leuten zu helfen, die arm und krank sind. **5** Gibt einen Teil deiner Reichtümer den Wohlfahrtseinrichtungen. **6** Ich gab das Trinken und das Rauchen auf.
S. 39	go on, go away, go on, gone out, go through, going off, goes with
S. 40	**1**d, **2**a, **3**c, **4**b
S. 43	**1** Hang your clothes up. Why don't you hang your clothes up? **2** Don't hang about all day long, do something. **3** Hang on to your plans. **4** Don't hang out of the window.
S. 45	**1** "Don't hold anything back." **2** "I hope your family will hold together." **3** "We were held up by the police." **4** "We were held up at the garage."
S. 46	**1** You should have your tonsils out. **2** Don't have the telly on all day. **3** You should hand your papers in. **4** I can help out if you want.
S. 47	**1** … join in. **2** … jot the number down. **3** jack the car up. **4** … jump off
S. 50	**1** keep up, **2** kept back, **3** keep … off, **4** keep on, **5** keeps to, **6** keep up with, **7** keep ourselves from, **8** keep away, **9** Keep … to, **10** keep down
S. 51	**1**d, **2**e, **3**b, **4**a, **5**c
S. 53	Du kannst alle Fragen mit *Yes, I do, / No, I don't* beantworten. Bei Frage 2 musst du natürlich einen Betrag nennen. Um die *phrasal verbs* zu üben kannst du aber auch in ganzen Sätzen antworten, zum Beispiel: **1** Yes, I lay some money aside each month.
S. 54	**1** He always leaves out lots of words in his letters. **2** You have left the signature and the date out. **3** Leave off making this noise, won't you? **4** Why do you leave all the hard work up to me? **5** Otherwise he might feel left out.
S. 56	**1** My mum/dad/sister/brother does. **2** I don't talk to him/her for a couple of days. **3** I ask him to tidy up the room. **4** No, I wouldn't. I would talk to his parents. **5** It depends./No, I wouldn't. Etc.
S. 58	**1** Ich habe so manche Hungersnot durchgemacht und ich habe so manchen Alptraum erlebt. **2** Ich habe gelernt, in schwierigen Situationen zurechtzukommen. **3** Als ich 12 war, musste ich von Zuhause weggehen. Wir Kinder konnten nicht von unseren Eltern leben. Wir waren zu viele. **4** Mein Vater lebte nur, um zu arbeiten. / Für meinen Vater war die Arbeit das Wichtigste. **5** Ich bin glücklich, dass ich in dieser netten Stadt mein Leben (zu Ende) verbringen kann.

S. 61	**1**b, **2**b, **3**a, **4**a, **5**a, **6**a, **7**b, **8**b, **9**a, **10**a
S. 62	Versuche echte Antworten zu geben. Oftmals kannst du mit Kurzantworten *Yes, I do* oder *No, I don't* antworten. Versuche aber auch lange Antworten zu formulieren, indem du die Frage aufgreifst.
S. 64	**1**b, **2**d, **3**a, **4**e, **5**c
S. 65	**1** … mix them up. **2** … marked them off. **3** … mix them up. **4** … marked them down. **5** … mark them down.
S. 67	**1**c, **2**e, **3**b, **4**d, **5**a
S. 69	**1** Hol' es ab! **2** Hol' sie ab! **3** Heb' sie auf! **4** Nimm ab!
S. 70	**1** Warum hört er nie auf, auf mir herumzuhacken? **2** Würdest du bitte die Dosen aufheben? **3** Lass mich in Ruh'. Lege dich mit jemandem Gleichstarken an. **4** Ich würde nachts niemanden auf der Straße im Auto mitnehmen.
S. 71	**1**d, **2**a, **3**e, **4**b, **5**c
S. 73	**1** push off, **2** push up, **3** push aside, **4** push over, **5** push around
S. 77	**1** Where shall I put these pictures up? **2** Somewhere in the kitchen. **3** Put your book aside and help me with the washing-up. **4** Why don't you use the dish-washer? **5** Have you put the rubbish out? **6** No, not yet (No, I haven't). I thought you've done that already. **7** Don't be so lazy. You've put on weight anyway. **8** That's not true. I've already put up the tent for the party in the garden. **9** Put the cups away in the cupboard. **10** I've done that already.
S. 78	**1** Ich wünschte mir, ihr würdet zu streiten aufhören. **2** Ich werde mich nicht wegen ein paar Pfund streiten. **3** Es besteht keine Notwendigkeit, darüber zu streiten.
S. 80	**3** – **1** – **2**
S. 82	**1** round off, **2** round off, **3** round up, **4** round up
S. 84	**1**, **2** Yes, I have. / No, I haven't. **3**, **4** Yes, I would. / No, I wouldn't. **5**, **6** Yes, I have. No, I haven't. **7** Yes, I would. No, I wouldn't.
S. 84	**1**c, **2**a, **3**b
S. 86	Individuelle Antworten, zum Beispiel: **1** Yes, I have often seen visitors off to the airport. / No, I have never seen visitors off to the airport **2** I can always see through my sister when she pretends to do something. Etc.
S. 87	individuelle Antworten
S. 89	**1** I was just setting up the Monopoly when I suddenly heard the alarm. **2** Somebody must have set off the alarm, I thought. **3** I ran out the room and I saw a burglar trying to get into the barn. **4** I threatened to set my dog on him. **5** When the man saw my dog he ran away. **6** Next morning I sat off early to report that to the police.
S. 91	**1** I'd like to settle down. **2** I settled in quickly at my new job. **3** Finally we settled on green. **4** It's hard to settle into this new way of life. **5** Settle down and listen. **6** Shall I settle up?

S. 93	**1** c, **2** d, **3** a, **4** b, **5** g, **6** e, **7** f
S. 94	**1** You shouldn't shut your dog up in the house for a long time. **2** You should shut off your music from time to time. **3** You shouldn't shut the dog out in cold weather. **4** You shouldn't say "Shut up!" to anybody. **5** You shouldn't shut your eyes to cruelty against animals.
S. 96	**1** b, **2** c, **3** a, **4** d
S. 98	**1** around/about, **2** back, **3** down, **4** out, **5** up
S. 100	**1** d, **2** b, **3** c
S. 102	**a** 10, **b** 4, **c** 7, **d** 3, **e** 9, **f** 5, **g** 1, **h** 2, **i** 6, **j** 8
S. 104	**1** g, **2** f, **3** a, **4** b, **5** d, **6** e, **7** c
S. 108	**1** Mutter hätte mir alle Süßigkeiten wegnehmen sollen. **2** Mutter hätte mich nicht jeden Tag mit dem Auto in die Schule bringen sollen. **3** Ich muss morgen zum Zahnarzt, der mir den letzten Zahn ziehen wird. **4** Ich kaufte gestern Abend ein neues Jackett. Der Laden wird es zurücknehmen, wenn es nicht passt. Es wird ohnehin nicht passen. **5** Ich kann mir die Stiefel nicht selbst ausziehen. Ich brauche Hilfe. **6** Ich hätte mit dem Joggen beginnen sollen. Ich hätte dann nicht so zugenommen. **7** Seit Ewigkeiten ist niemand mehr mit mir ausgegangen. Niemand mag mich. **8** Die Bücher müssen morgen zurückgegeben werden. Ich sollte sie in die Bibliothek zurückbringen, aber ich bin zu müde.
S. 110	**1** Wende dich nie zu früh an die Eltern. Besprech die Dinge zuerst mit den Kindern. **2** Erlaube den Kindern nicht freche Antworten zu geben. **3** Sprich niemals herablassend zu den Kindern. **4** Rede nicht um den heißen Brei, wenn du etwas erklärst. **5** Versuche sie nicht zu überreden, sondern von deiner Ansicht zu überzeugen.
S. 112	**1** The dog. **2**. The thieves. **3** A little boy. **4** The workmen from the telephone company.
S. 114	**1** of, **2** of, **3** about / of , **4** of, **5** aloud, **6** through / over, **7** over, **8** up
S. 116	**1** … throw it out. **2** … throw them away. **3** … throw him out. **4** … threw them back even more. **5** … throw it up. **6** … throwing in your remarks all the time.
S. 118	**1** b, **2** c, **3** a, **4** c, **5** a
S. 120	**1** c, **2** e, **3** f, **4** d, **5** a, **6** b
S. 122	**1** on, **2** off, **3** out, **4** in, **5** off
S. 124	**a** Schreibe bald! **b** Hast du mich schon abgeschrieben? **c** Ich vergaß, deine Telefonnummer aufzuschreiben. Ruf' mich an. **d** Oder fällt dir nichts ein, worüber man schreiben könnte?